Illustrators:
Sue Fullam
Agnes Palinay

Editor:
Dona Herweck Rice

Editorial Project Manager;
Karen J. Goldfluss, M.S. Ed.

Editor-in Chief:
Sharon Coan, M.S. Ed.

Art Director:
Elayne Roberts

Cover Artist:
Sue Fullam

Imaging:
Alfred Lau

Production Manager:
Phil Garcia

Publishers:
Rachelle Cracchiolo, M.S. Ed.
Mary Dupuy Smith, M.S. Ed.

Cooperative Learning Activities for Language Arts
Intermediate

Authors:
Grace Jasmine
Julia Jasmine, M.A.

Teacher Created Materials, Inc.
P.O. Box 1040
Huntington Beach, CA 92647
©1995 Teacher Created Materials, Inc.
Made in U.S.A.

ISBN-1-55734-651-8

The classroom teacher may reproduce copies of materials in this book for classroom use only. The reproductions of any part for an entire school or school system is strictly prohibited. No part of this publication may be transmitted, stored, or recorded in any form without written permission from the publisher.

Table of Contents

Introduction 3
Overview 4
Preparation
    Selecting Cooperative Groups 5
    Parent Introduction Letter 10
    Whole-Classroom Readiness and Activities 11
    Assessment and Portfolios 25

The Past
    Dinosaurs 28
    Cave Dwellers 34
    The First Farmers 38
    Ancient Egypt 46
    Ancient Greece 53
    Ancient Rome 57
    Middle Ages 62
    Explorers 66

The Present
    "The History of Time Travel" Play 70
    Clocks 71
    Dictionary of Time 79
    Time Out for Role-Plays 84
    Time Management 88
    Time of My Life 102
    Beat the Clock 106
    Time Line Mural 109

The Future
    A Note to the Teacher About the Writing Process 113
    Providing a Knowledge Base 115
    Establishing a Need to Write: Making a Time Capsule 118
    Brainstorming: My Message to the Future 120
    Organizing Ideas 123
    Writing and Sharing the First Draft 130
    Peer-Editing, Revising, and Rewriting 133
    Completing the Time Capsule 134
    Publishing the Time Capsule 136
    Other Publishing Ideas 138

Cooperative Learning Award 142
Answer Key 143

Introduction

Welcome to the wonderful world of cooperative learning! *Cooperative Learning Activities for Language Arts* contains new, exciting, and relevant cooperative learning activities that relate to the past, the present, and the future.

A Complete Resource Book

This book provides everything you need to present a language arts unit using cooperative learning activities. It includes not only innovative ideas but also practical suggestions and blackline masters to help you put the ideas into action in your classroom.

The first sections explain how to make cooperative learning a part of your curriculum. They include an overview, instructions and activities for introducing cooperative learning to your students and parents, guidelines for setting up groups, ideas for an activity center, and suggestions for assessment and portfolios.

The rest of the book provides a wide range of cooperative activities divided into three parts.

> **The Past** centers around exploration of times past. Student groups will visit dinosaurs, explore ancient civilizations, meet historical figures, and more.
>
> **The Present** explores time. Students will manage time, make clocks, set goals, and work with calendars. They will explore the language of time and take imaginary time trips to exciting places.
>
> **The Future** focuses on the writing process. Each activity features a specific step in the process. The students will take and record a fantasy trip into the future and publish their work in a variety of ways.

Easy to Use

This book is designed with the busy teacher in mind. Each activity unit includes a complete lesson plan which explains the **purposes** of the unit, the **skills** to be taught, and the **materials** that are needed.

The **procedures** for teaching the unit are described in detail. Ways to **simplify** the unit are provided. These suggestions allow you to adapt the activity to beginning cooperative learners or to shorten the activity to fit into a tight schedule. Ways **to expand** the unit are also provided to challenge advanced students and to continue a lesson that needs further development.

The lesson plan for each activity unit ends with suggestions for **evaluation** and **processing**.

Overview

Cooperative Learning Activities for Language Arts begins the path of language arts discovery. The book is geared for children who have some experience with cooperative learning, though certainly it can be adapted for the beginner.

To begin a school year or to make a smooth transition into cooperative learning from a more traditional classroom, the book begins with a series of whole-class activities. After you feel your class is ready to break into time-travel teams, it is easy to begin. The format is a simple one. Starting with the past, students begin to discover the world of long ago. Next, students explore their own concepts of time in the present day. Finally, student teams design and create a time capsule for the future while working through each step of the writing process.

Beginning the Book

To begin cooperative learning on a successful note, focus on the whole-class activities on pages 14–21. In this way, students can begin to interact as a class and then in pairs in a nonthreatening and positive environment.

These activities will help you build an attitude of friendliness and cooperation in your classroom before attempting to organize student groups. Additionally, whole-class and pair activities will provide you with opportunities for assessing individuals to best determine the members of each group. (See "Selecting Cooperative Groups," pages 5–9.)

Cooperative Learning Groups

This book has been written for a classroom with thirty students, or six groups of five. Simply add or subtract groups, or students in a group, to best serve your class's particular needs. Remember, in cooperative learning, it is best to use an uneven number of students in each group whenever possible.

What About Results?

One of the best reasons for introducing cooperative learning activities throughout the curriculum is that children benefit from them in distinctly observable ways. After completing the activities in this book, look for student improvement and mastery in the following areas:

- ❖ Oral presentation
- ❖ The writing process
- ❖ Cognitive and high-order learning skills
- ❖ Communication and conflict-resolution skills
- ❖ Self-esteem
- ❖ Ability to work with classmates
- ❖ A better understanding of time and history

A Final Note

The ultimate goal of *Cooperative Learning Activities for Language Arts* is to provide interesting and exciting cooperative learning experiences for each of your students. Enjoy your exciting journey through the wonderful world of language arts!

Preparation

Selecting Cooperative Groups

Picture This

It is day one of a new school year. Mrs. Sumersover walks shakily into her classroom and gazes out at the sea of expectant, childish faces. She feels stressed. She would like to add cooperative learning to her program this year, but she is not really sure how to do it. Most of her experience has been in traditional classroom settings. She spent the summer at the beach reading information on cooperative learning, but she still feels unsure and uncomfortable. She does not have tenure, the economy is in recession, and she cannot afford to make any mistakes. At the same time, other teachers have already successfully incorporated cooperative learning into their classrooms. Mrs. Sumersover needs assistance from a friendly, clear, nonthreatening source.

I Need a Vacation

Most of us are not this worried about how to incorporate current teaching trends into our classroom, but many of us have shared Mrs. Sumersover's sense of dread. Mrs. Sumersover needs a clear, concise, stress-free, and entertaining resource to help her pull her classroom and her curriculum together.

Icing on the Cake

Ms. Beterthanu walks to her classroom on the first day of school. Eyes follow her. How does anyone who teaches manage to look that put together? She opens the door to her classroom with satisfaction. A giant fabric palm tree rises from the center of the room. Gleaming computers shine in a neat row against the wall, keyboards smiling, anticipating little fingers. In one corner, a wooden reading area built to look like a real house stands like a monument to learning. How nice to have a handy husband!

Top of the Class

She just needs one more thing: a cooperative learning plan as well-prepared and nifty as her adorable classroom. She needs cutting-edge materials to make her curriculum sparkle as much as her room. She is a professional and a perfectionist, and she has to have the best.

Making It Happen

Maybe you know both of these teachers. Both of them could benefit from streamlined, easy, effective ways of incorporating cooperative learning into their classrooms successfully—the first time. The following section gives you quick and easy guidelines to help you set up your cooperative learning classroom. Blackline master forms have been included whenever possible to streamline the process.

Preparation

Selecting Cooperative Groups (cont.)

Kinds of Learners

While all children are different, and certainly children's abilities and skill levels can change, most students fit into one of these four categories of learners:

- ❖ High Achievers
- ❖ Special Needs Students
- ❖ English as Second Language (ESL) Students
- ❖ Competent Achievers

When selecting the members of cooperative groups, be sure to create a mix of all four areas. To help determine the members of each cooperative group, the following descriptions offer some easily recognizable qualities that learners of the same type share.

High Achievers

High achievers can fall into two categories. Current educational thought holds that while some students are considered high achievers based on their I.Q.s, others are labeled this way not so much because of exceptional intelligence but because of exceptional motivation. When looking for the high achievers, consider these qualities:

- ❖ High I.Q.
- ❖ Good verbal skills
- ❖ Good oral communication skills
- ❖ Problem-solving ability
- ❖ Good study and concentration skills
- ❖ Academic excellence
- ❖ Interest in learning
- ❖ Leadership skills
- ❖ Exceptional talent
- ❖ Multifaceted interests and abilities

While there are certainly other ways to determine high achievers, and not all high achievers share the same qualities, this partial list will help you know what qualities to consider. High achievers can bring ideas, leadership, and assistance into a cooperative group.

Special Needs Students

While special needs students can be high achievers, low achievers, ESL students, or English speakers, the commonality is that they all need special assistance. Some may have difficult family situations, like a divorce or separation, while others may be diagnosed with severe emotional or behavioral problems. While the special needs student requires extra care, placing him or her in the right situation just might diminish or solve his or her problem. A sad, distracted child might be placed in a group with a lively, happy child, thus giving that child a model for growth. Children, like adults, benefit from the positive attitudes of those around them. Look for these qualities when determining your special needs students:

- ❖ History of emotional or behavioral problems
- ❖ Anger
- ❖ Low level of socialization skills
- ❖ Recovery from a recent illness
- ❖ Attention Deficit Disorder (A.D.D.)
- ❖ Recent family upset
- ❖ Low motivation
- ❖ Quick to yield to frustration
- ❖ New to the country, state, city, or school

While there are other things that may contribute to a child's place in the special needs category, these qualities will give you a guiding framework. Remember that this group, more than any of the others, is transitory. It is very possible during the length of a school year for a child's situation to change enough for removal from or addition to this category.

Preparation

Selecting Cooperative Groups (cont.)

English as a Second Language (ESL) Students

ESL students are usually challenged by the circumstances of their learning. Most of us have no idea how traumatic it is to be relocated to a new country with little or no knowledge of the language, the customs, the culture, or the people. Moreover, often these students are without friends, having left their old ones behind.

ESL students come in every variety under the sun. Some are extremely well educated in their own language, learn English quickly, and assimilate with relative ease. Others have frightening, painful experiences when it comes to success in their new schools.

ESL students have a special place in this book, one that will help you to help them bring their own cultures into the learning experience. Rather than being ostracized for their differences, ESL students will be able to assume the role of "cultural diplomats." It is the intention of this book to support multicultural awareness and education wherever possible. By its very content, *Cooperative Learning for Language Arts* will make the challenge of working successfully with ESL students a little easier.

When looking for those to classify as ESL students, be aware of the following qualities:

- ❖ Recently arrived from another country
- ❖ American-born, but in a home where a language other than English is predominant
- ❖ Speaks English well, but has not mastered reading or writing in English
- ❖ English-speaking, but under the care of one for whom English is a second language
- ❖ Stuck in the "silent interval" of language acquisition

Once provided with the special attention they need, ESL students often turn out to be competent or high achievers. The cooperative learning activities in this book will help you to gain access to the strengths of these students and to provide them with many self-esteem-building opportunities.

Competent Achievers

Unfortunately, competent achievers, often those who "do not give any trouble," often get very little teacher attention. In a classroom with thirty or more children, it is the competent child who is "all right" and gets left to fend for himself or herself. When singling out competent achievers in your classroom, remember that these children should be rewarded and not penalized for being less demanding. Those with behavior problems should not see their negativity reinforced by the focus always remaining on them. Furthermore, in every group of competent achievers, there are a number of hidden high achievers who will blossom with the proper self-esteem-building attention and experiences.

When looking for competent achievers, watch for the following signs:

- ❖ Students whom you do not often think about
- ❖ Average grades
- ❖ Oral and written language skills around grade level
- ❖ Shyness or quietness
- ❖ Pleasant low-key personalities
- ❖ Low resistance to the learning experience
- ❖ A marked willingness to follow

While not all competent achievers fit this mold, it is safe to say that these are the children you are likely to think about less than any of the others. They are the children who patiently stand in lines, raise their hands, and rarely cause any disturbances. Competent achievers are the people who keep the world running smoothly, in and out of the classroom, and for this they deserve much praise and loving hugs.

Preparation

Selecting Cooperative Groups (cont.)

Now What?

Now that you know what to look for in determining the different learning types in your classroom, use the blackline master on page 9 to simplify the process. In this book, your cooperative groups will become time-travel teams.

As far as group size is concerned, five is a good number. Therefore, if you have thirty students, you will create six groups, each consisting of five individuals. In cooperative learning situations, an uneven number is an asset during the decision process. (No hung jury, so to speak!) When selecting the members of each group, here is what to remember:

The "Salad Bowl"

Rather than as a melting pot, a situation in which everyone's individual traits melt together, the ideal cooperative learning situation should be thought of as a salad bowl. In a salad bowl, all ingredients (individual learning types) mix together. They create synergy while remaining individuals. For purposes of explanation and ease, follow this simple recipe:

Cooperative Learning Salad Bowl

Combine the following ingredients:

- High achievers
- Special needs students
- ESL students
- Competent achievers

Select five according to taste. Flavor with the following random differences:

- Genders
- Personality types
- Ethnicities
- Learning styles

Introduce each ingredient into the mix slowly, stirring in large pieces of humor, understanding, cooperation, and support. Let the mix remain together—qualities, strengths, and weaknesses intermingling. Facilitate ingredients rising to the occasion . . . and enjoy the results!

#651 Cooperative Learning Activities for Language Arts ©1995 Teacher Created Materials, Inc.

Preparation

Selecting Cooperative Groups (cont.)

Legend
- HA: High Achiever
- SN: Special Needs Student
- ESL: English as a Second Language Student
- CA: Competent Achiever

Group One (*example*)

(HA)

(CA)

(CA)

(SN)

(ESL)

Notes: _____
_____
_____

Group Two

( )

( )

( )

( )

( )

Notes: _____
_____
_____

Group Three

( )

( )

( )

( )

( )

Notes: _____
_____
_____

Group Four

( )

( )

( )

( )

( )

Notes: _____
_____
_____

Group Five

( )

( )

( )

( )

( )

Notes: _____
_____
_____

Group Six

( )

( )

( )

( )

( )

Notes: _____
_____
_____

©1995 Teacher Created Materials, Inc. #651 Cooperative Learning Activities for Language Arts

Preparation

Parent Introduction Letter

Dear Parents,

In our classroom this year, we will be approaching language arts in a very interesting way. We will be studying the various aspects of time and time travel. While doing so, every student will have a chance to work cooperatively in pairs or in groups. This will give everyone a chance to take part in many enriching learning experiences.

Here is where you come in. Cooperative learning is a special kind of learning. Rather than sitting in a chair all day and learning solely by rote, your child will be working in small groups. He or she will have the chance to receive more personalized attention while learning how to interact effectively with peers. Also, as our subject for this unit is language arts, there will be a real emphasis on the mechanics of writing clear sentences and paragraphs, ending with a published whole-class effort.

Because of this different way of learning, parent volunteers are very important. If you have several, or even a few, hours a week that you would like to spend in your child's classroom, it will be a wonderful help to the class and will be a very fond memory for your child.

I realize, of course, that most of you have extremely busy schedules and that some of you will not be able to take part in our classroom. However, there are many ways to take part in your child's learning experience, and I would be happy to speak with you about how you can become involved. Thank you for your support!

Sincerely,

_____

If you would like me to call you, please fill in the information below and send it to me.

Name: _____

Child's Name: _____

Phone: _____

Preparation

Whole-Classroom Readiness and Activities

Easing into Cooperative Learning

Prepare your students for cooperative learning by conducting whole-class cooperative activities. Whole-class activities are especially conducive to creating a comfortable, safe environment in which students have some knowledge and understanding of one another. It is helpful to ease into the cooperative experience since many students may never have had the experience of cooperative interaction.

Parallel Players and Pre-Cooperative Learners

The students in your classroom probably have some experience in cooperative learning. However, children at any skill level or age who have not been exposed to cooperative learning often make a slow transition. Early childhood education experts tell us that the younger the children in a group are, the less comfortable they will feel with group participation. Most toddlers and preschool age children parallel play. This means that they play near each other at separate tasks. It is important to note that children *learn* to play together. It is not their initial instinct.

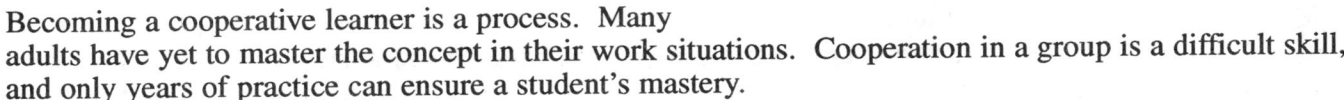

Becoming a cooperative learner is a process. Many adults have yet to master the concept in their work situations. Cooperation in a group is a difficult skill, and only years of practice can ensure a student's mastery.

To ease into cooperative learning, focus on pre-cooperative learning skills. Teachers can focus on the idea of children learning how to get along within the classroom setting. Concepts such as sharing and taking turns are understood by pre-cooperative learners, and while a pre-cooperative learner may not always feel comfortable sharing or taking turns, these ideas are ones they will certainly recognize.

Finally, be aware of your students. When they have had enough of a cooperative activity, turn to a less stressful and more autonomous one.

Partner Activities

Cooperation is an important component in any classroom. When children cooperate, they have the opportunity to think about and assimilate new ideas.

Use the whole-class activities on page 12 to nurture the cooperative atmosphere within your classroom. Each activity is followed by a suggested partner activity. To help ease your students into the concept of cooperative learning, allow them this time to work with one partner only. The first section of this book focuses on pre-cooperative activities and partner activities within the cooperative group to help you ease your children into cooperative learning. You may wish to have your students become very comfortable with partner activities before beginning the cooperative activities in the rest of the book, or you may find it beneficial to use both group and partner activities, depending on your students' learning needs.

©1995 Teacher Created Materials, Inc.

Preparation

Whole-Classroom Readiness and Activities (cont.)

1. **Personal Journal**

   This activity can be used for individual and partner interaction. Have each child start a journal. When any classroom activity ends, have the children draw and write about the activity. Each journal entry can be dated with a notation about the activity to which it refers.

   Let the students know that this journal is for them. There is no one right way to do it. It is just for fun. They can look back on it and remember what they did in class and how they felt about it.

   Partners

   Assign a partner to each child. Partners will discuss their journal entries. This activity will not only help children relax in a cooperative learning environment, but it will also build cooperative and communicative skills in a nonthreatening way.

2. **Rest and Remember**

   This activity will help children prepare for or unwind after a classroom activity or special event. Have the children go to their seats or rest their heads on their desks. You may wish to dim the classroom lights or play soft music. While the students are resting, ask them to think about the activity they just completed. Ask them to picture the activity, see it as a mental movie, and decide what they liked and did not like about it. Ask them how they felt—happy, sad, angry, excited, etc. Ask them what they would like to do differently next time they work in their groups. You may then wish to follow up by reading the students a short, happy poem or story.

   Partners

   Have students talk with a partner immediately following the "Rest and Remember" exercise, discussing what they liked about the activity they have just completed. This can also be another opportunity to use their journals.

3. **Letter Home**

   This activity is helpful in encouraging language and memory skills. It also engenders parental and parent/child participation in your program.

   Have students write and illustrate what they did in their cooperative learning activity. Use the form on page 13 or have students create their own. Students can then take their letters home.

   Have the students return the letters and share what their parents thought about the activity and their participation. This activity will also help you to stay in contact with parents consistently, rather than just when there is a problem.

   Partners

   Have partners view each other's letter home and make one positive comment or compliment. This activity encourages students to support each other, and it promotes self-esteem.

Preparation

Whole-Classroom Readiness and Activities (cont.)

Dear _____,
Here is a description of what my cooperative group did today.
I helped my group by:
_____
_____
_____

My favorite part was:
_____
_____
_____

                              Love,
                              _____

- -

Parent Comments:
_____
_____
_____

Note from the Teacher: Thank you for supporting your child in his/her cooperative learning experience. I welcome all parent volunteers. Please write your number here if you would like a phone call.

                              Thank you,
                              _____

Name: _____
Name of Child: _____
Phone: _____

Preparation

Whole-Classroom Readiness and Activities (cont.)

Use the following activities to build the students' interest in the idea of time travel. You may wish to use these as beginning team activities to build cooperative skills.

1. **How to Build a Time Machine**

    A time machine is easy and fun to build. Just let your imagination be your guide. Here is what you will need:

    - a large refrigerator box
    - poster paints
    - enlarged copies of the time machine controls on pages 17–19
    - lots of imagination

    Make your time machine so that time travelers can stand or sit inside and use the controls. See the sketches below for some suggestions. You may wish to have the students participate in building the machine or prepare it in advance (as a surprise) so that it is ready on Monday morning as they arrive.

    After the time machine has been completed, have the students do the activities on page 15 to acquaint themselves with the cooperative process.

Preparation

Whole-Classroom Readiness and Activities (cont.)

2. **Time Traveler Membership Card**

   Have each student color the card (page 20) and prepare it for time travel. Students should fill in all information except for their team name. At the first meeting of their team, they will fill in this name. Then, have students draw a picture of themselves or glue a small class picture in the upper right hand corner. Use clear contact paper to laminate the finished cards. Explain to the students that these will be their passports to time travel.

3. **Time Travel Passport**

   The time travel passport (pages 21–22) will be an interesting way for students to see how they have grown and changed from the beginning of the year to the end. It is also a report card of sorts. Some teachers will use it to communicate with parents. Others will have students take it home at the end of the year or keep it on their desks for Open House. The choice is yours.

   To prepare passports, reproduce and distribute pages 21–22. Have the students fold each page back along the dashed lines from top to bottom and then forward in half again from side to side. The name-and-team page should go first. Pages 5–8 of the completed activities list should follow page 4 of the same list. Staple the two sections together along the side of the passport.

   Begin this whole-class activity by discussing passports and their use. Explain that the passport will contain two Polaroid® pictures of the student—one taken at the beginning of the year and one taken at the end. (Students will be able to see how they have changed.)

   Each time an activity has been completed, have the students add it to the list of completed activities. You may wish to note special comments here, such as "a job well done." Have the children work with partners to discuss their passports after an activity has been completed.

4. **Time-Travel Instruction Books**

   This partner activity will help build cooperation and teamwork between partners. Select partner pairs. Give each pair time to look at the time machine thoroughly. Use the time-travel instruction book forms on pages 23–24 to have the students write, proof, and make a final draft for a time-travel instruction book.

   Remind students that they must give clear instructions on how to use this time machine, just like those they would find enclosed with a new game or toy. Select the top three instruction books for a class vote. The class can choose the best one to be placed inside the time machine.

   If time permits and the students are interested in other time machine activities, use some of the suggestions on page 16.

©1995 Teacher Created Materials, Inc.   #651 Cooperative Learning Activities for Language Arts

Preparation

Whole-Classroom Readiness and Activities (cont.)

5. **Time Machine Ideas**
   A. Have students create time-travel brochures for their favorite destinations.
   B. Create a flight simulator. To do so, have the children record an audio version of their imagined sounds of flight. Use sound effects and lots of imagination.
   C. Let students use their time machine for a think tank. They can go inside the time machine and read, dream, or plan new activities.
   D. Have a time machine party. Let the students come as their favorite characters from the past, present, or future.
   E. Watch science-fiction films or videos that apply to the topic of time travel.
   F. Have students write their own science-fiction stories.
   G. Have students write or tell about artifacts they have found in imaginary time-travel journeys.
   H. Have students dress as their favorite historical figures and plan and present speeches for the rest of the class.
   I. Have students draw pictures of space creatures or write about them in "My Day with a Space Creature."

Whole-Classroom Readiness and Activities — Preparation

Time Machine Controls

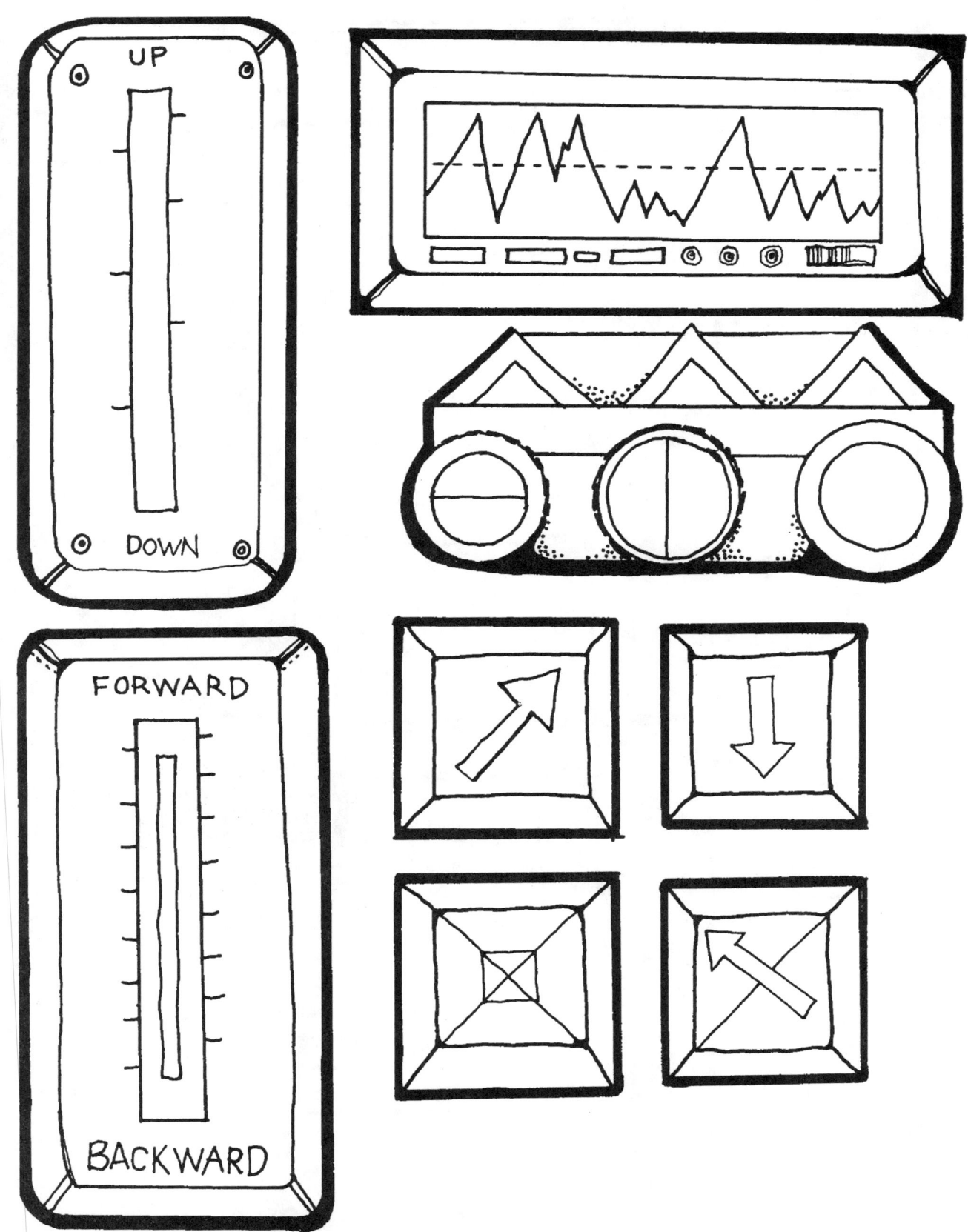

Preparation *Whole-Classroom Readiness and Activities*

Time Machine Controls (cont.)

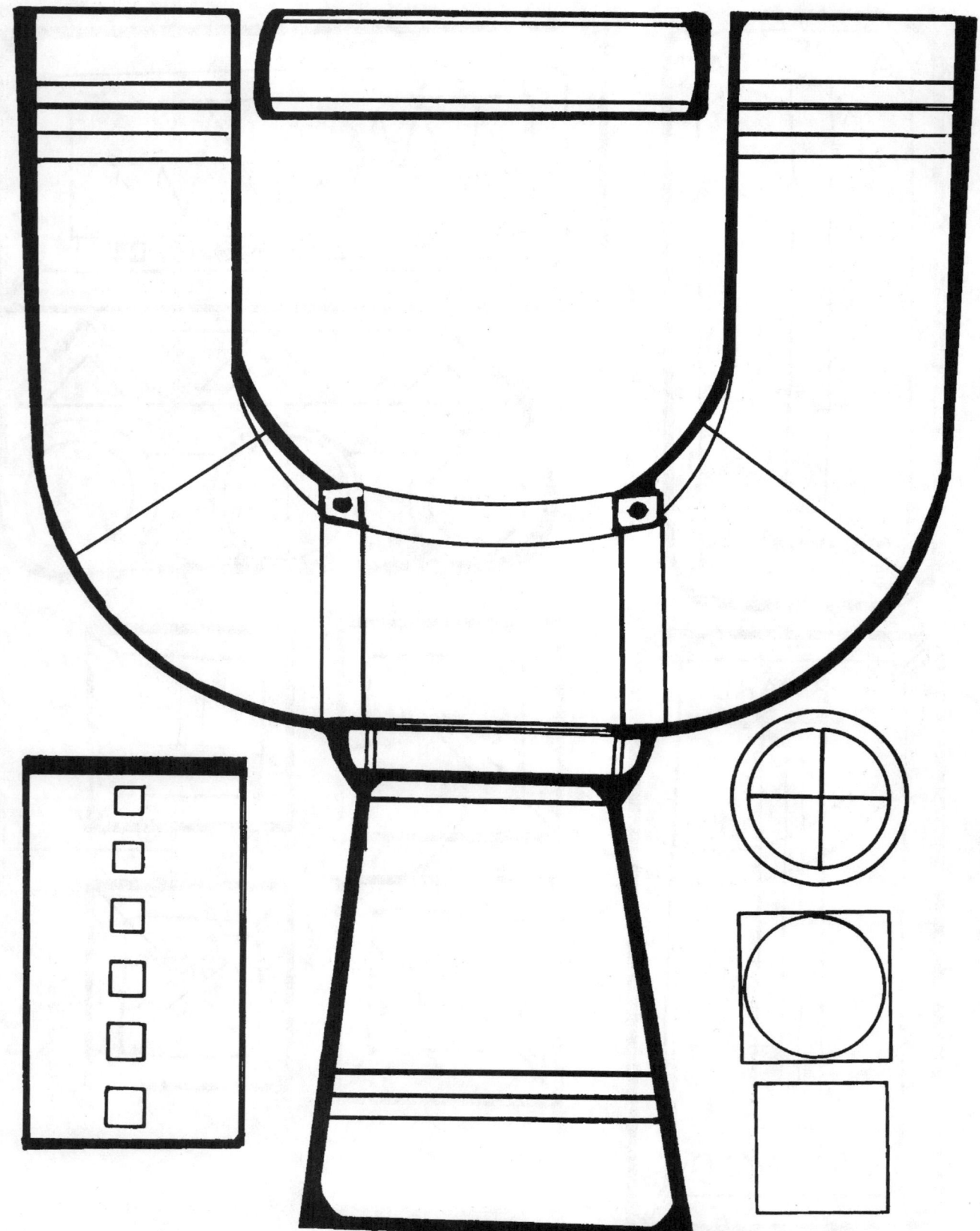

Whole-Classroom Readiness and Activities — *Preparation*

Time Machine Controls (cont.)

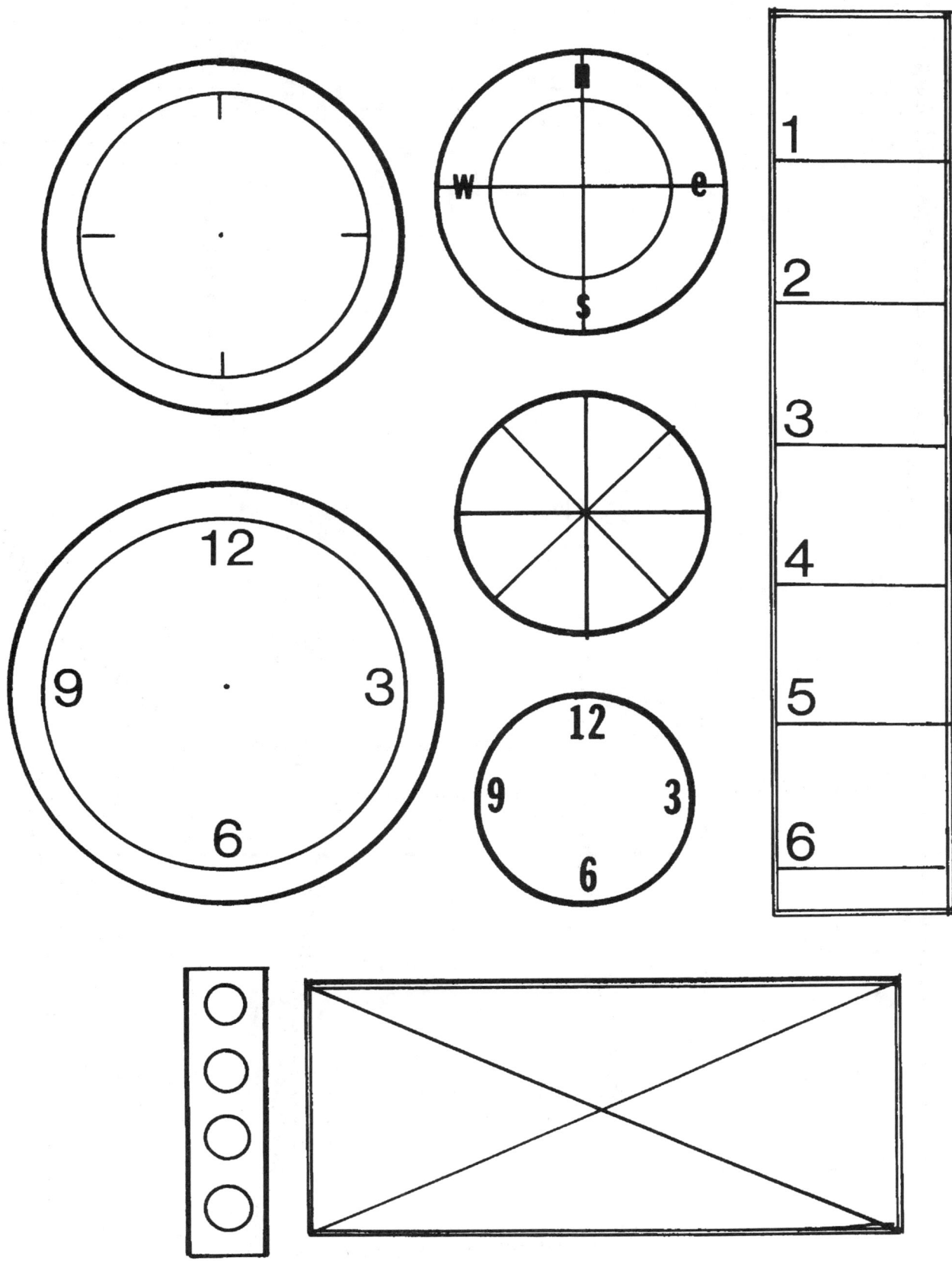

©1995 Teacher Created Materials, Inc. — #651 Cooperative Learning Activities for Language Arts

Preparation   *Whole-Classroom Readiness and Activities*

Membership Cards

Time Travel Member Place photo here. Name _____ Team _____	**Time Travel Member** Place photo here. Name _____ Team _____
Time Travel Member Place photo here. Name _____ Team _____	**Time Travel Member** Place photo here. Name _____ Team _____
Time Travel Member Place photo here. Name _____ Team _____	**Time Travel Member** Place photo here. Name _____ Team _____

Whole-Classroom Readiness and Activities — **Preparation**

(page 2 and page 3 are printed upside-down at the top of the sheet)

page 3

Photo #2 _____ Date _____

page 2

Photo #1 _____ Date _____

Completed Activities	Comments
_____	_____
_____	_____
_____	_____
_____	_____
_____	_____
_____	_____
_____	_____
_____	_____
_____	_____
_____	_____
_____	_____
_____	_____

page 4

Passport

Name _____

Team _____

©1995 Teacher Created Materials, Inc. — 21 — #651 Cooperative Learning Activities for Language Arts

Passport (cont.)

page 8

Completed Activities	Comments

page 7

Completed Activities	Comments

Completed Activities	Comments

page 5

Completed Activities	Comments

page 6

Whole-Classroom Readiness and Activities — *Preparation*

Time-Travel Instruction Book

by

_____

Preparation   *Whole-Classroom Readiness and Activities*

Time-Travel Instruction Book (cont.)

This is how to use your new time machine:

_____

_____

_____

_____

_____

_____

_____

_____

_____

_____

_____

_____

_____

_____

_____

_____

_____

_____

_____

_____

Preparation

Assessment and Portfolios

Make It Manageable

Assessing your students' progress does not have to be a formidable task. Included for you here are two handy forms to lighten the load and consolidate your efforts. First, there is the "Individual Anecdotal Record" on page 26. Use this to keep a daily record of individual student progress in each activity or area. Be sure to date these records and to include them in a student portfolio. For more information and other forms, refer to Teacher Created Materials' *Portfolios and Other Assessments*.

Next, you will find "Reflections on the Activity" on page 27. This form is for students to fill out after each activity. This form will help you gauge how the students are doing and how they feel about the activities.

A Word About Portfolios

Create portfolios out of small boxes or shirt gift boxes, something that can stack but at the same time is big enough for bulky projects. It is important when assessing your students by the portfolio method to make parents aware that they will not receive as much take-home work. It is always a good idea to make parents aware of your assessment process and make them part of it at the very beginning of the year. Inform them every step of the way, and you will save yourself some big headaches. You may even gain some interested and wonderful parent helpers!

Assessment and the Pre-Cooperative Learning

Finally, remember that cooperative learning is a difficult concept. Preschoolers and some primary children prefer, and are far better at, parallel play. The transition is usually a slow one. Keep in mind that it is a process, and adjust your expectations accordingly.

Have Fun!

This book has been designed with the idea that not only will your students like the activities and have a good time, but so will you. Choose activities that you really love. Do not feel you have to do them all or that you must do them exactly as described. Coupled with your own creativity, the activities in this book will equal a fabulous year. Good luck!

Preparation

Assessment and Portfolios (cont.)

Run off a stack of these forms and keep them—one for each student in your class—in a three-ring binder. Make your notes right on the appropriate form. When a page is filled up, it can be replaced with a new page and the filled page placed in the student's portfolio. No time is lost transcribing information!

Individual Anecdotal Record

Name _____

Date	Comment

Preparation

Assessment and Portfolios (cont.)

Run off copies of this form for your students to use as they start the process of reflecting on their own achievements. This particular form was designed for primary children and requires little writing. Allow plenty of time for the children to look over and think about their work. When the form has been completed, attach it to the work (if possible) and include it in each student's portfolio.

Reflections on the Activity

Name _____ Date _____

When I look back on the work I have done, I feel . . .

_____
_____
_____
_____
_____

I have become better in . . .

_____
_____
_____
_____
_____

I am really proud of . . .

_____
_____
_____
_____

Next time I do an activity like this, I will . . .

_____
_____

©1995 Teacher Created Materials, Inc.   #651 Cooperative Learning Activities for Language Arts

The Past

Dinosaurs

Purpose: to develop a sense of prehistoric time; to use group skills such as cooperation and compromise, oral language skills such as listening and speaking, and thinking skills such as analysis and synthesis

Skills: applying information and logic to the construction of a visual representation of time; applying knowledge of parts of speech to a sentence-building game; listening; teamwork; reading comprehension; the ability to follow directions

Materials: copies of pages 29–33 (one per student or group); writing and coloring supplies; the classroom time machine (page 14)

Procedure: Adjust the time machine controls for 170 million years ago. Then, begin the activity by having a class discussion about dinosaurs. When did they live? Where? Did people live at the same time? Have the students consult reference books to compare the age of the earth with the time period when the dinosaurs lived and the time period in which human beings appeared.

Next, challenge the class to consider how they might represent these facts. How might they draw a "picture" that will clearly show a time scale as big as this? Have the students go to their cooperative learning groups to discuss this challenge and come up with a suggestion.

Reconvene as a large group and have a representative from each group present the group's idea. Comment on the thinking that was done. Then, introduce the worksheet on page 29 as one way to represent the time scale. Have students go back to their groups, complete the worksheet, discuss the sample time scale, and compare the worksheet with their own ideas.

Next, if there is time, allow the students to complete the activity on page 30. If you run short of time, let the students take the activity home and check it in their groups on the following day. You might also partially fill in the blanks before duplicating them to simplify the activity. (See the answer key on page 143.) Walk around the room to help and answer questions while the students are working together.

At the next meeting, work with partners or in groups to review page 31. Then do the activity on pages 32–33. Meet as a whole class to discuss the activity.

To Simplify: Skip the research and challenge and go directly to the worksheets. Have the students work together to discuss the first worksheet and complete the second and third.

To Expand: Ask students to create their own parts-of-speech activity and try to stump the other members of their groups.

Evaluation: Evaluate this activity by observing and listening to the students as they interact in their groups. Make any appropriate notes on the anecdotal record forms (page 26). These can later be put in the students' portfolios along with the completed worksheets.

Processing: Process with the whole class by having the groups report on what they did to complete the assignment and what they might do differently if they did it again. What was the hardest part of this assignment? Which part of the assignment was the easiest?

Dinosaurs *The Past*

Name_____

Time Scale

Here is one way to represent the age of the earth and the relationship between the time when the dinosaurs lived and the appearance of people on the earth.

The age of the earth is estimated at approximately 4,000,000,000 (4 billion) years. If this time is represented by the hour shown on the face of a clock, each of the 60 minutes represents about 66 $^2/_3$ million years. Dinosaurs appeared during the Jurassic Period which started about 170 million years ago and lasted 40 million years. People arrived in the last few seconds before the hour ends.

Discuss with your partner or group how, on the clock below, you could represent the time periods spanning the age of the dinosaurs and the appearance of people on earth. (The clock represents the age of the earth.) Use a light-colored marker to color in the Jurassic Period. Draw a line with a fine-line, dark-colored marker to show when people arrived.

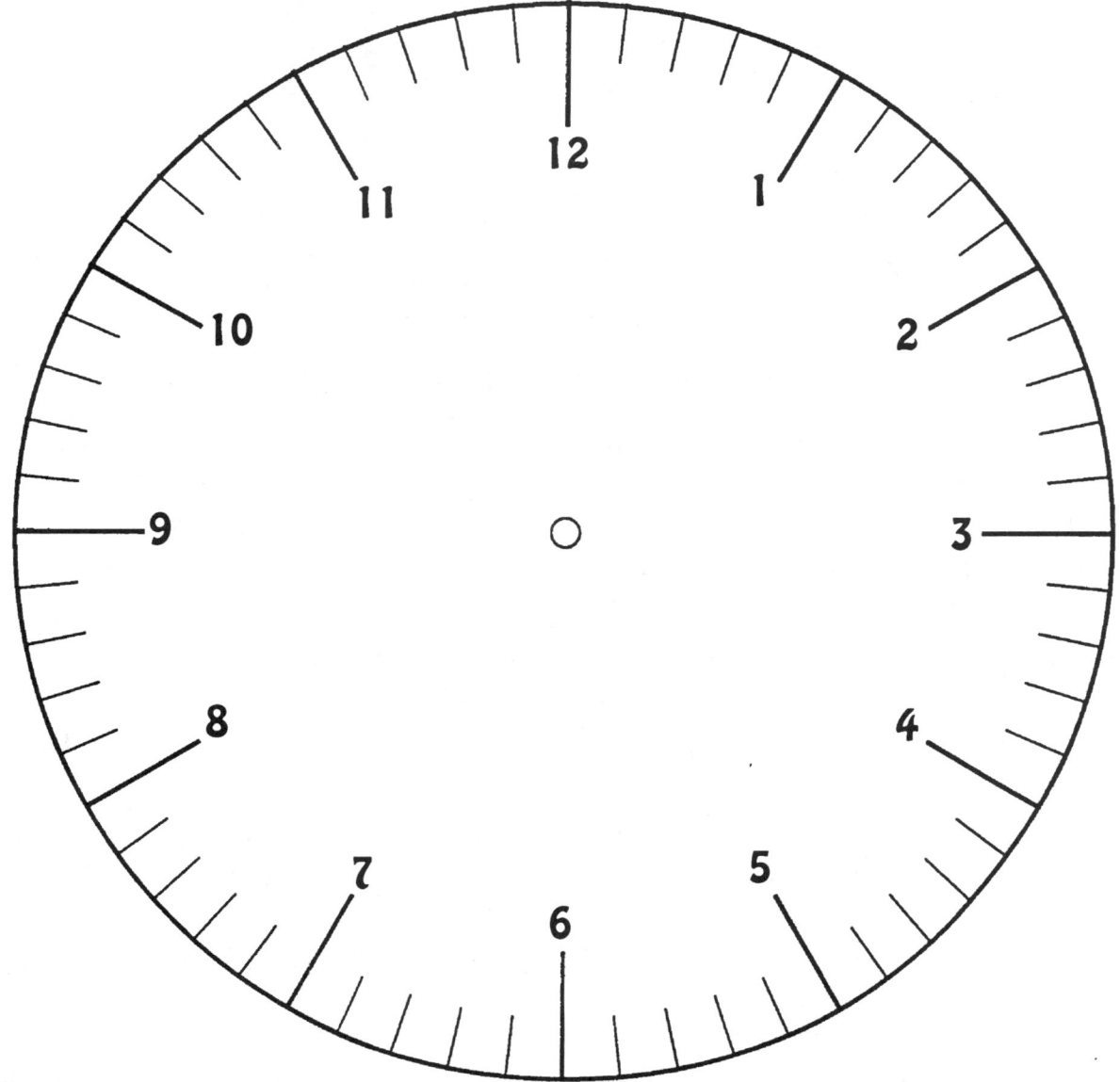

The Past   *Dinosaurs*

Name_____

Dinowords

Use the "dinoword" bank at the bottom of the page to fill in the blanks in the sentence skeletons.

1. _____ _____ _____ _____ _____ _____
    common noun   verb   proper noun   verb   adverb   adverb

2. _____ _____ _____ _____
    proper noun   verb (to be)   article   common noun

3. _____ _____ _____
    proper noun   verb (to be)   adjective

4. ___ ___ ___ ___ ___ ___ ___
  pronoun   verb   preposition   common noun   preposition   possessive pronoun   common noun

5. ___ ___ ___ ___ ___ ___
  common noun   verb (to be)   adjective   preposition   adjective   common noun

6. ___ ___ ___ ___ ___ ___ ___ ___ ___ ___
 article   adjective   common noun   verb   common noun   verb (to be)   article   common noun   preposition   common noun

7. ___ ___ ___ ___ ___ ___ ___ ___ ___ ___ ___
 article   common noun   preposition   adjective   common noun   verb (to be)   adverb   adjective   preposition   adjective   common noun

"Dinoword" Bank

interesting	very	theory	the	very
people	extinct	herbivore	from	carnivorous
says	of	learn	Allosaurus	know
about	ran	study	most	became
were	reasons	we	fossils	unknown
is	the	dinosaurs	scientists	dinosaurs
was	for	their	birds	of
dinosaurs	a	ancestors	was	prehistoric
fast	Stegosaurus	animals	Tyrannosaurus Rex	
an	new	to		

#651 Cooperative Learning Activities for Language Arts   30   ©1995 Teacher Created Materials, Inc.

Dinosaurs The Past

Fossil Formations

With your partner or group, read and discuss the following information about how fossils are formed. Together, complete the activity on pages 32 and 33.

How Fossils Are Formed

Scientists who study things left from life long ago are called paleontologists (pay-lee-on-TAHL-o-jists). Many fossils from plants and animals have been found all over the world. The remains of plants and animals that have turned to stone over millions of years tell us what life was like back then. Fossils can tell us much about dinosaurs except their colors and habits. Most scientists think that dinosaurs were much the same color as reptiles today.

Skin Prints: Fossilized skin prints from some dinosaurs show that their skin was rough and covered with scales. Other prints show some dinosaurs were covered with fur or feathers.

Bones: Bone fossils are reassembled to show many things about dinosaurs. Scientists can tell where muscles were connected to the bones, how the dinosaurs moved, and whether they walked on two or four feet. The bones show how many fingers or toes were on their hands or feet and what kinds of claws they had. The height, length, and weight of dinosaurs are also determined by the bones.

Skull: The skull shows the size of the dinosaur's brain. A larger brain usually indicates a smarter animal. The teeth from the skull show the kinds of foods the dinosaur ate. The eye sockets are measured to show the size of the eyes and where they were located on the dinosaur's head. Large eyes set at the front of the skull provide better eyesight than small eyes and those located on the sides.

Bony Parts: Some dinosaurs had bony structures on parts of their bodies. The frills of the Ceratopsian dinosaurs, the plates of the Stegosaurus, and the heads, tails, fins, and sails of other dinosaurs were all made from hard, bone-like material. Scientists believe that these structures could have been used to regulate body temperature, to provide protection, or simply to tell male from female.

Tail: The bones from the tail of a dinosaur show how long it was and how the tail was used. Most dinosaurs held their tails out from their bodies for balance. Some dinosaurs used their tails as weapons and could swing them from side to side as well as move them up and down.

Footprints: The footprints left by dinosaurs support the belief that they lived in herds. Footprints of many dinosaurs walking together have been discovered all over the world. The footprints show that the young dinosaurs walked along with the grown ones and indicate that dinosaurs took care of their young.

Fossil Formation: Dinosaur fossils were formed when a dinosaur died and was covered with deep layers of sand or dirt. As water seeped through the place where the dinosaur was buried, minerals replaced the body tissue which slowly turned to stone. Millions of years later, when the sand and dirt were washed away, the dinosaur fossil was uncovered. When fossils are discovered, scientists carefully dig them out and send them to a museum to be studied.

The Past *Dinosaurs*

Fossil Formations (cont.)

Activity Directions

Materials:

activity sheet (page 33), word blocks (below), crayons or markers, scissors, glue, 9" x 12" (23 cm x 30 cm) construction paper

Directions:

1. Color the pictures on the worksheet.
2. Cut out the pictures and the word blocks.
3. Put the pictures in order to show how fossils are formed.
4. Glue the pictures in order onto the construction paper.
5. Match the word-block sentences to the correct pictures and glue them in place.
6. Put the title "How Fossils Are Formed" at the top of the pictures. Put your names on the back of the paper.

Word Blocks

Heavy wind and rain washed away part of the sand and dirt. Part of the dinosaur fossil could be seen.	The bones were hidden for millions of years. Water and minerals seeped through the sand and dirt, slowly turning the bones to stone.
A scientist found the fossil of the dinosaur and carefully dug it out of the stone to take it to a museum for study.	The bodies of some dinosaurs were covered by sand and dirt after they died.
All the dinosaurs died suddenly 65 million years ago.	Dinosaurs lived on Earth for 160 million years.

Dinosaurs *The Past*

Fossil Formations (cont.)

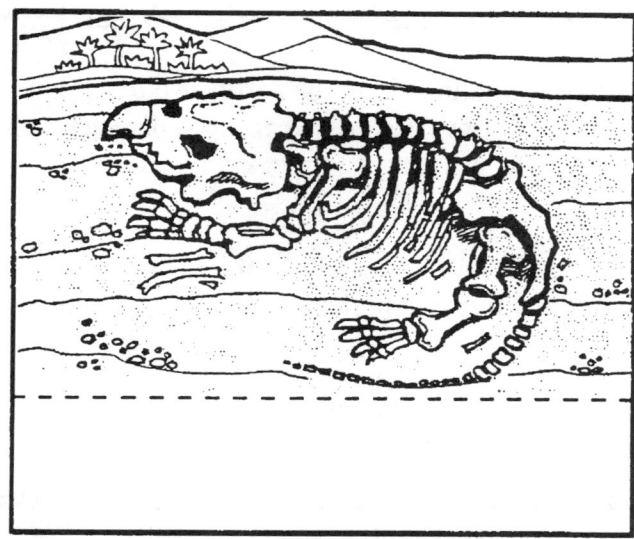

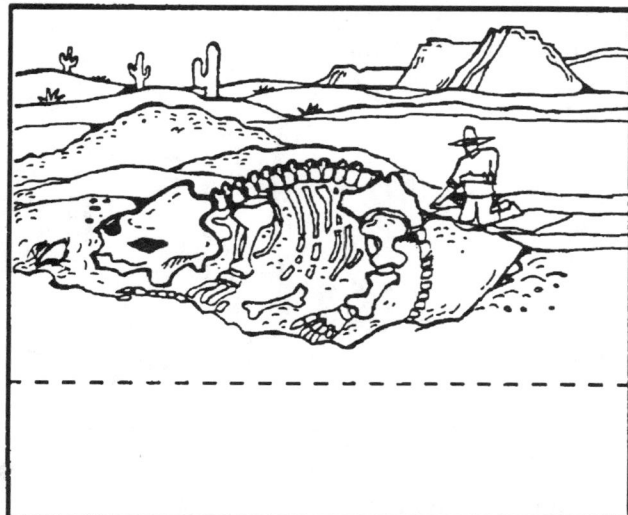

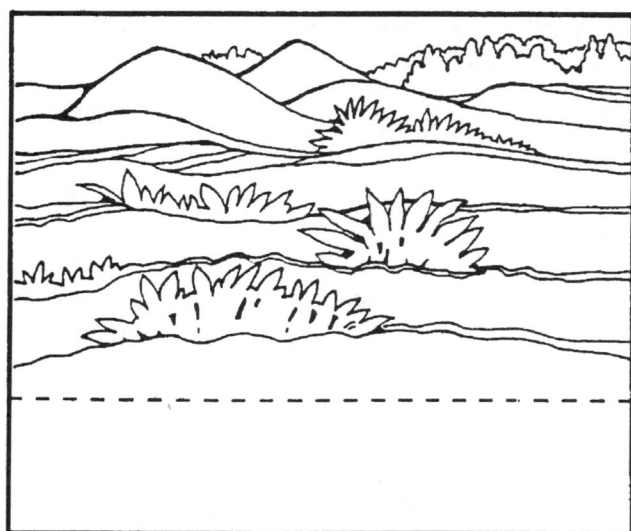

The Past

Cave Dwellers

Purpose: to acquire and give artistic expression to information about the early cave dwellers; to compare life today with the life probably lived by cave dwellers; to use group skills such as cooperation and compromise, oral language skills such as listening and speaking, and thinking skills such as analysis and synthesis

Skills: application of information and logic for the creation of a diorama; ability to display information on a chart; listening; teamwork; writing; reading comprehension; ability to follow directions; use of art materials

Materials: writing materials; miscellaneous art materials such as construction paper, scissors, paints, brushes, and glue; shoeboxes; sample dioramas; copies of pages 35–37

Procedure: Begin the activity by giving the whole class information about cave dwellers. You can read aloud to the class, provide books at grade level, and show movies and videos. Then, take a class vote to determine an appropriate time at which to set the time machine controls.

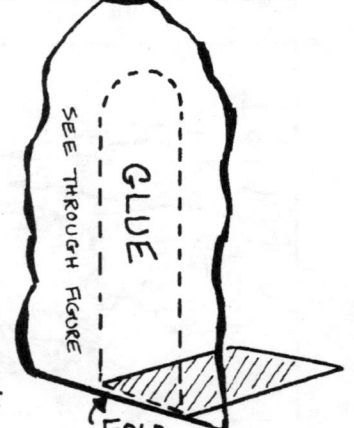

Display sample shoebox dioramas. You might make these or show some saved from another class.

Tell the students they will be going to their cooperative learning groups to complete two tasks. Each group will create a diorama showing some aspect of the life lived by the cave dwellers. They can design and draw their own or use the suggestions and patterns on pages 35 and 36. Then, each group will complete a chart (page 37) comparing and contrasting the information they have gathered about cave dwellers with what they know about modern life. This worksheet will help them to focus on particular areas. As the students are working, walk around the room to help and answer questions.

Reconvene as a large group and have representatives of each group present the group's diorama and chart. Encourage the class to ask questions and make positive comments.

To Simplify: Concentrate on the dioramas. Have students compare and contrast orally as part of the whole-class discussion.

To Expand: Ask students to add more categories to the chart.

Evaluation: Evaluate this activity by observing and listening to the students as they interact in their groups. Make any appropriate notes on the anecdotal record forms (page 26). These can later be put in the students' portfolios along with the completed worksheets.

Processing: Process with the whole class by having the groups report on how they decided on and split up the jobs. How do they feel about the product they created? What might they do differently if they did it again? What was the hardest part of this assignment? What was the easiest part?

Cave Dwellers

The Past

Diorama Suggestions and Patterns

Color the figures, cut them out, and mount them on cardboard. Glue stands to their backs.

caveman

cave woman

caveperson stand

caveperson stand

wooly mammoth

wooly mammoth stand

©1995 Teacher Created Materials, Inc.

#651 Cooperative Learning Activities for Language Arts

The Past   *Cave Dwellers*

Diorama Suggestions and Patterns (cont.)

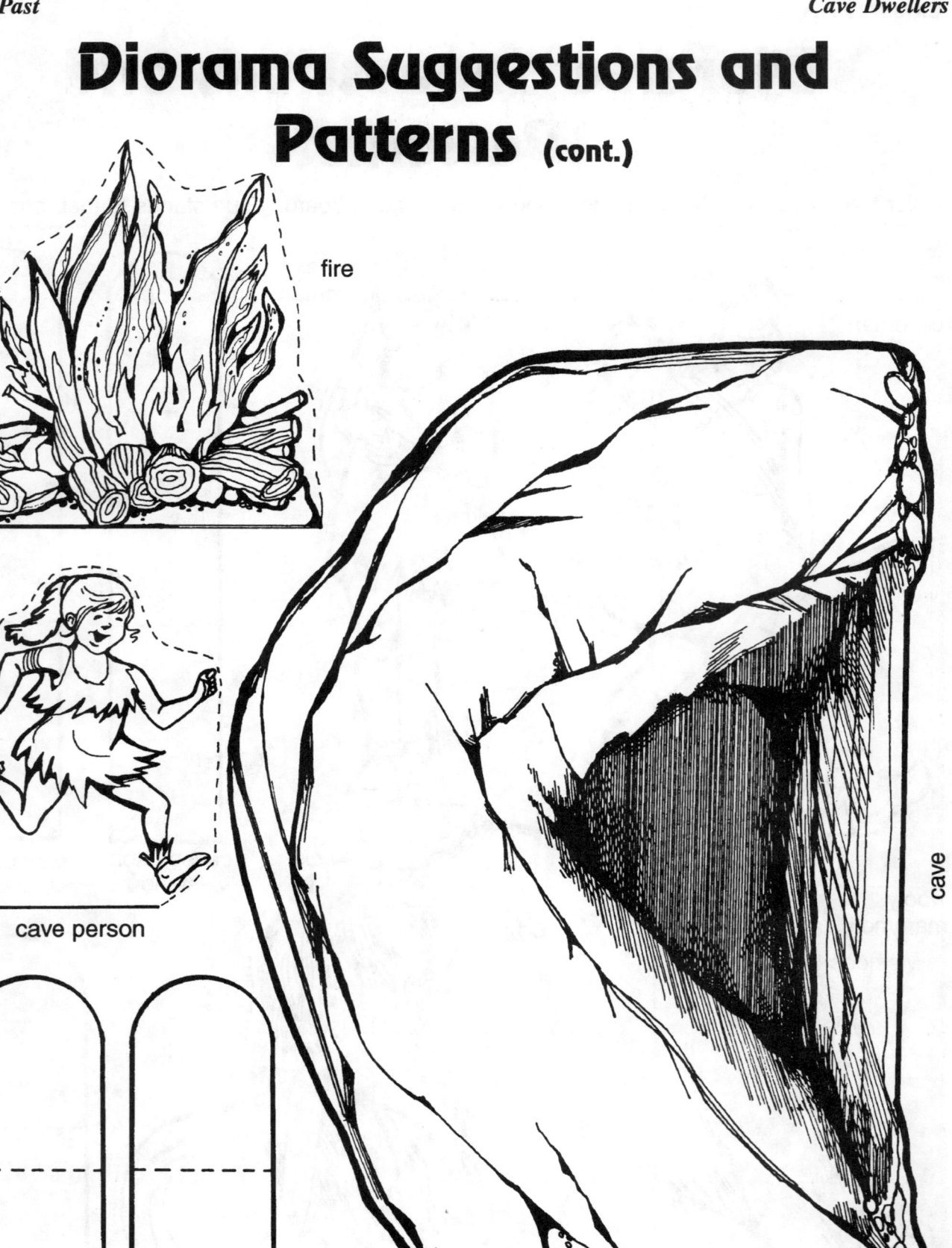

fire

cave person

stands

cave

#651 Cooperative Learning Activities for Language Arts   ©1995 Teacher Created Materials, Inc.

Cave Dwellers *The Past*

Name_____

Compare and Contrast Chart

Fill in the boxes to complete the chart.

	Cave Dwellers	**People of Today**
Dwellings		
Clothing		
Getting Food		
Kinds of Food		
Methods of Cooking		
Transportation		
Tools and Weapons		

©1995 Teacher Created Materials, Inc. #651 Cooperative Learning Activities for Language Arts

The Past

The First Farmers

> **Purpose:** to learn about the development of agriculture; to investigate the relationship between the domestication of plants and animals; to develop map skills
>
> **Skills:** map reading; research; reading comprehension; oral communication (both speaking and listening); writing
>
> **Materials:** task cards (pages 39–44); map (page 45); reference materials, including sets of encyclopedias and books and videos about early civilizations

Procedure: Begin the lesson as a large group. Remind students of the hunting and gathering lifestyle of the cave dwellers. Ask if anyone knows how or when people began to grow their food. Ask what the relationship might be between beginning to grow food and beginning to tame and raise animals. Tell students the following: Each group will be responsible for a specific area of research, you will give each group task cards on which to write their answers and extra cards on which to consolidate their findings, and they will come together to report their findings at the end of the lesson. The task cards can be posted on a bulletin board illustrated by the students. Point out the location of the reference materials. When students have gone to their groups, answer questions and give help as needed. As soon as a group finds the information that tells how long ago these things happened, they should send a representative to set the dial in the classroom time machine.

(If students would like to view one or more videos, you might want to do this on the first day of this activity while still in the whole group. If there are not enough reference materials to go around, spread this activity over several days, giving the members of each group a special time when only they have access to the materials.)

To Simplify: Read aloud to the whole class one or more books about early civilizations. Have a class discussion before students begin their cooperative work.

To Expand: Distribute the maps (page 45) and have students label the rivers and mark the locations they find in their research. Students can also draw pictures illustrating early agriculture.

Evaluation: Evaluate the students' cooperative group skills while they are working. Evaluate the groups' completed task cards when they report to the class. Make appropriate notes on the anecdotal record forms (page 26), which can later be added to the students' portfolios.

Processing: Process with the whole class by having each group report the results of its research as recorded on the task cards. Ask students questions like the following: What is the most interesting thing you learned? What is the most surprising thing? Would you have preferred to be a cave dweller or one of the first farmers?

The First Farmers *The Past*

Task Card One: Domesticated Animals

Decide which member of your group should answer each question below. Then, use reference books to find the answers to the questions. When everyone has completed his or her research, put all of your answers together on the extra copy of this sheet. Answer the "Group Question" together. Be ready to report to the class.

Group Members:

_____   _____   _____

_____   _____   _____

_____   _____   _____

1. Why did people want to domesticate (tame) animals?
   _____
   _____

2. Where did they get the animals they domesticated?
   _____
   _____

3. What did people use the animals for?
   _____
   _____

4. Do people today keep domesticated animals?
   _____
   _____

5. What do people today use domesticated animals for?
   _____
   _____

Group Question:

How would you go about domesticating an animal? Describe the process. (Write your answer on the back of this paper.)

The Past *The First Farmers*

Task Card Two: Domesticated Plants

Decide which member of your group should answer each question below. Then, use reference books to find the answers to the questions. When everyone has completed his or her research, put all your answers together on the extra copy of this sheet. Answer the "Group Question" together. Be ready to report to the class.

Group Members:

_____   _____   _____
_____   _____   _____
_____   _____   _____

1. Why did people want to grow plants?
   _____
   _____

2. Where did they get the plants they began to grow?
   _____
   _____

3. How did people take care of the plants?
   _____
   _____

4. What did people use the plants for?
   _____
   _____

5. What do people use plants for today?
   _____
   _____

Group Question:

How would you go about domesticating a plant? Describe the process. (Write your answer on the back of this paper.)

The First Farmers *The Past*

Task Card Three: Where and Why

Decide which member of your group should answer each question below. Then, use reference books to find the answers to the questions. When everyone has completed his or her research, put all your answers together on the extra copy of this sheet. Answer the "Group Question" together. Be ready to report to the class.

Group Members:

_____   _____   _____

_____   _____   _____

_____   _____   _____

1. Where did agriculture start?
   _____
   _____

2. Why did it start where it did?
   _____
   _____

3. What do plants need in order to grow?
   _____
   _____

4. What different things did people do with what they grew?
   _____
   _____

5. What other things did people need to help them make good use of what they grew?
   _____
   _____

Group Question:

What kinds of plants did people probably grow first? (Write your answer on the back of this paper.)

©1995 Teacher Created Materials, Inc.   #651 Cooperative Learning Activities for Language Arts

The Past *The First Farmers*

Task Card Four: The Effects of Agriculture

Decide which member of your group should answer each question below. Then, use reference books to find the answers to the questions. When everyone has completed his or her research, put all your answers together on the extra copy of this sheet. Answer the "Group Question" together. Be ready to report to the class.

Group Members:

_____   _____   _____

_____   _____   _____

_____   _____

1. How did agriculture affect where people lived?
   _____
   _____

2. How did agriculture affect what people lived in?
   _____
   _____

3. How did agriculture affect people's diets?
   _____
   _____

4. How did agriculture affect the division of work between men and women?
   _____
   _____

5. Did religion have any connection with agriculture?
   _____
   _____

Group Question:

What effect do you think agriculture had on people's health? (Write your answer on the back of this paper.)

The First Farmers   *The Past*

Task Card Five: The First Cities

Decide which member of your group should answer each question below. Then, use reference books to find the answers to the questions. When everyone has completed his or her research, put all your answers together on the extra copy of this sheet. Answer the "Group Question" together. Be ready to report to the class.

Group Members:

_____   _____   _____

_____   _____   _____

_____   _____   _____

1. What are the names of the first cities?

2. Where were they located?

3. What does agriculture have to do with the first cities?

4. Did everyone in the first cities grow his or her own food?

5. What new "professions" are connected with the development of cities?

Group Question:

What laws would have been needed in the new cities? (Write your answer on the back of this paper.)

The Past *The First Farmers*

Task Card Six: The New Leisure

Each member of your group should research one activity described below. Use reference books to research the activities. When everyone has completed his or her research, put all your findings together on the extra copy of this sheet. Answer the "Group Question" together. Be ready to report to the class.

Group Members:

_____ _____ _____

_____ _____ _____

_____ _____ _____

Name and describe five activities that were not practical before the development of agriculture and cities:

1. _____
   _____
   _____

2. _____
   _____
   _____

3. _____
   _____
   _____

4. _____
   _____
   _____

5. _____
   _____
   _____

Group Question:

Why did people have more leisure after the development of agriculture? (Write your answer on the back of this paper.)

#651 Cooperative Learning Activities for Language Arts ©1995 Teacher Created Materials, Inc.

The First Farmers *The Past*

First Farmers Outline Map

Label the rivers. Mark and label any important landmarks you discover while doing your research.

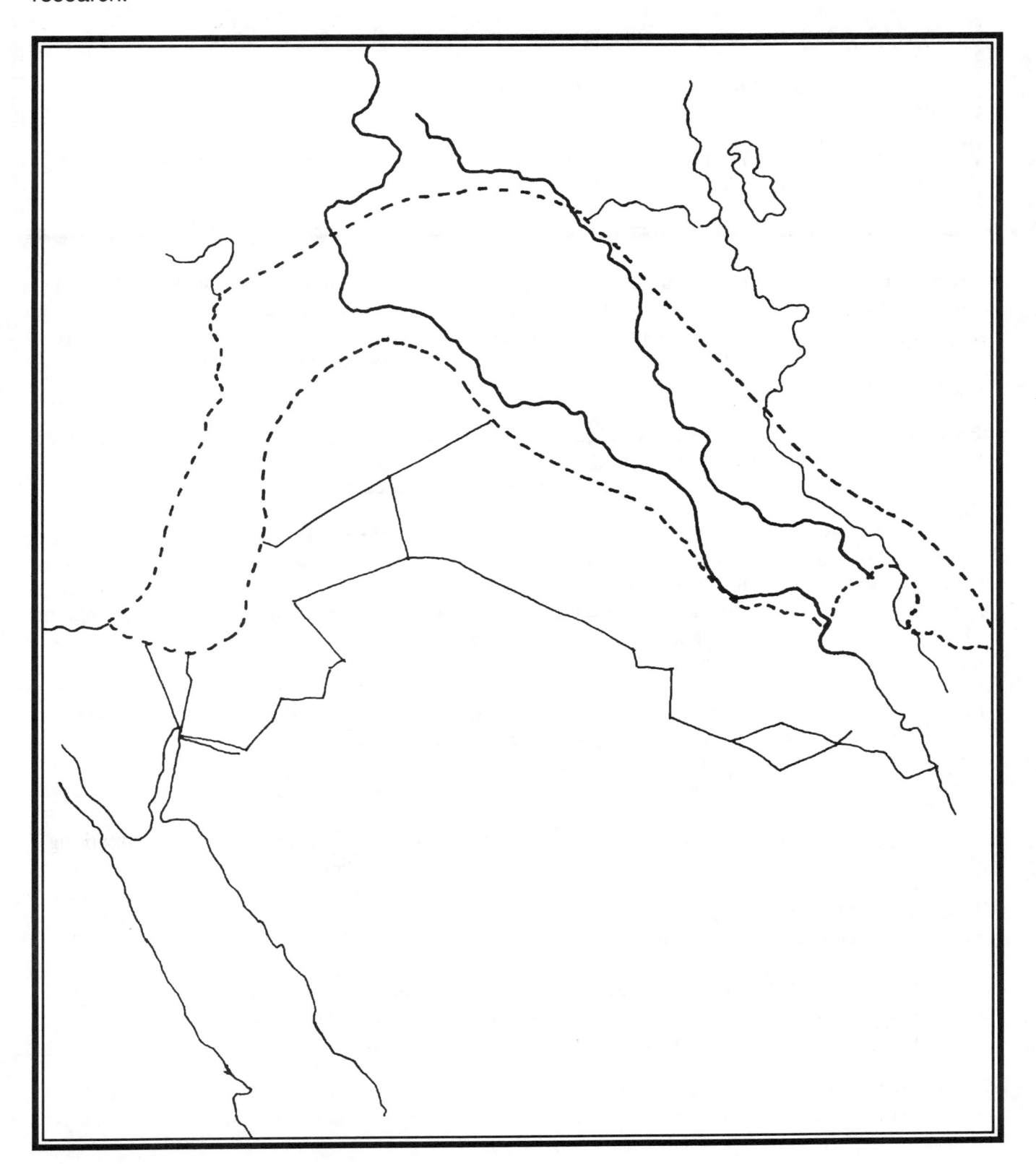

The Past

Ancient Egypt

> **Purpose:** to learn about and practice the kinds of writing used in a newspaper; to develop and use cooperative learning skills; to acquire information about ancient Egypt
>
> **Skills:** reading and listening comprehension; oral and written communication; creative expression
>
> **Materials:** pages 47–52; writing and drawing materials; reference materials, including sets of encyclopedias, books, and videos about ancient Egypt

Procedure: If you have been studying ancient Egypt, you can cover this activity quickly, or you can decide to make it a culminating activity for your unit on Egypt. If the information about Egypt will be new to your students, you will probably want to spend some time reading books and viewing videos before beginning to write. (These same techniques can, of course, be used in any area of the curriculum.)

Begin the writing part of the lesson as a large group. Discuss the different kinds of writing that appear in a newspaper. Have students identify examples in a real newspaper. ("Writing Tips" on page 51 describes five kinds: news stories, feature stories, editorials, obituaries, and comic strips.)

Tell students they will be producing their own newspaper about Egypt. Each group will need a "Group Agenda" (page 52) so the members of each group will remember to (1) brainstorm the subject matter for each type of writing and (2) assign a different type to each group member. Group members will (3) produce a first draft, (4) edit each other's work, and (5) copy their work on paper divided into columns. (You may want to meet as a whole group after step one in order to prevent duplications in subject matter.)

Meet as a large group to share work. You may want students to cut apart their columns and paste up the newspaper, or you may want to do it yourself, adding headlines and color.

This makes a very interesting display for Open House.

To Simplify: Brainstorm ideas and make writing assignments in the large group. Collect all writing after step three and edit it yourself before passing it back to be recopied.

To Expand: Make each group responsible for pasting up a page. If you have a group left over, the members can make headlines and illustrations.

Evaluation: Evaluate the students' cooperative group skills while they are working. Evaluate the students' writing when they share it with the class. Make appropriate notes on the anecdotal record forms (page 26), which can later be added to the students' portfolios.

Processing: Process with the whole class by discussing and enjoying the completed newspaper. Ask them what they liked best and what they liked least. Also ask which part was easiest and which was hardest.

Ancient Egypt *The Past*

Handy First Draft Form

Write your first draft on the lines below.

Name _____ Date _____

_____
_____
_____
_____
_____
_____
_____
_____
_____
_____
_____
_____
_____
_____
_____
_____
_____
_____
_____
_____
_____
_____
_____
_____
_____
_____

Ancient Egypt

©1995 Teacher Created Materials, Inc.   #651 *Cooperative Learning Activities for Language Arts*

The Past *Ancient Egypt*

Paste-up Form I

Copy your edited work in columns below. Place "Paste-up Form II" under this form to keep your lines neat and straight.

Name _____ Date _____

Ancient Egypt *The Past*

Paste-up Form II

Put this form under "Paste-up Form I" to keep your lines neat and straight.

Name _____ Date _____

The Past   *Ancient Egypt*

Cartoon Form

Draw four different cartoons or one comic strip in the boxes on this page.

Name _____ Date _____

Ancient Egypt   The Past

Writing Tips

Newspapers contain several very different kinds of writing. Five kinds are explained below.

News Stories

News stories are supposed to be completely factual. The key words that will help you write a news story are WHO, WHAT, WHERE, WHEN, and WHY.

Early this morning	*firefighters in helicopters*	*dumped water*
When	Who	What

in the foothills	*to keep the brush fire from spreading.*
Where	Why

Feature Stories

Feature stories are mainly factual, but they contain lively and/or emotional details and some opinions.

Before taking off, the firefighter rubbed his smoke-reddened eyes and wondered when he would have his next meal, shower, or good night's sleep.

Editorials

While editorials may contain a foundation of facts, they really focus almost entirely on the opinions of their authors. They are written to persuade or convince the reader.

The recent local fires have made it clear to all thinking people that we must build more reservoirs to hold extra supplies of water for emergencies.

Obituaries

Obituaries, or death notices, are short biographies written about a person who has recently died. The more important or famous the person was, the more detailed the obituary.

Dr. Thomas Jackson passed away last weekend as the result of a skiing accident in Colorado. He will be missed by the children to whom he gave two days a week at Children's Hospital as well as by the patients in his private practice.

Cartoons

In general, there are two kinds of cartoons in the newspaper: **political cartoons** that point out current events and **comic strips** that both show and tell the adventures of their characters. Comic strips are usually created to be funny while political cartoons may be more thought-provoking than humorous. (Find examples of both kinds of cartoons in your newspaper.)

The Past   Ancient Egypt

Group Agenda

1. Brainstorm subject matters for each type of writing and record your decisions on the chart below.

2. Assign each group member a type of writing and record their names on the chart below.

Type of Writing	Subject	Group Member
News Story		
Feature Story		
Editorial		
Obituary		
Cartoon		

3. Write individual first drafts.

4. Peer edit.

5. Copy edited drafts on "Paste-up Form I." See the directions on the form (page 48).

The Past

Ancient Greece

Purpose: to develop an understanding of and appreciation for myths both as a form of literature and as an expression of ancient Greek culture; to write an original myth

Skills: reading and listening comprehension; oral and written communication; thinking skills, including analysis, synthesis, and evaluation; artistic skills

Materials: books with collections of myths and books with single myths and beautiful illustrations; books of legends, fables, and folktales from other countries and time periods; pages 54–55; writing and drawing materials including crayons, markers, and paints

Procedure: Read aloud myths, legends, fables, and folktales to the whole class for a week or two preceding this activity. Ask for comments that clarify the purpose of each story.

Start the activity itself with a class discussion in which students consider the similarities and differences they have noticed. (Myths tell how something began or why it happened. Additionally, Greek myths usually pertain in some way to their gods and to people as they relate to the gods. Because students will probably have a very limited knowledge of the Greek gods, you may want to expand the writing assignment to include fables and folktales.) Once students have a grasp of myths and their purpose, assign them to write original myths of their own.

Have students write their first drafts independently and go to their cooperative groups both to share their work and to do peer editing. Students should produce final drafts of their edited stories and illustrate them. If you plan to make multiple books, copy the pages before color is added and have students add color later. Publish by compiling the illustrated stories into a book for the classroom library. Give copies to other classes and to the school library.

To Simplify: Read to the students "How the Bear Got Its Stumpy Tail" or a similar story. Have the students write stories following this formula: "How The_____ Got Its _____."

To Expand: Have students read and then illustrate each other's stories. How close did the illustrator come to what the author had in mind? Have the groups discuss.

Evaluation: Evaluate cooperative learning skills by observing students as they work in their groups. Evaluate writing by using an appropriate rubric which can be placed in the portfolio with a copy of the story. (See page 56 for a sample rubric.)

Processing: Process with the whole class by having the students read their own stories aloud and react to the stories of others. Ask students to consider this question: Why did the ancient Greeks create myths?

The Past   **Ancient Greece**

Myth Form

Copy your edited myth on the lines below and on the next page. Use the space at the top of this page to illustrate your story.

Name _____ Date _____

Myth Form (cont.)

Sample Rubric

Use this rubric to evaluate the myth.

Score 3: High Pass

Student . . .

- responds to prompt.
- demonstrates noticeable evidence of organizational skills (e.g., strong opening and conclusion).
- demonstrates mastery of conventions (grammar, usage, mechanics, spelling).
- expresses interesting ideas and uses lively language.

Score 2: Pass

Student . . .

- responds to prompt.
- demonstrates adequate evidence of organizational skills (e.g., opening and conclusion).
- demonstrates use of conventions that do not inhibit reader's understanding.
- demonstrates understanding of language through use of appropriate vocabulary.

Score 1: Needs Revision

Student . . .

- may not respond to prompt.
- demonstrates little or no ability to organize material.
- does not use conventions correctly; reader's understanding is inhibited.
- uses inappropriate vocabulary.

Score 0: No Response

The Past

Ancient Rome

Purpose: to develop the ability to write questions and answers that are correctly categorized and reflect accurate information; to build a knowledge base of facts about ancient Rome

Skills: reading and listening comprehension; oral and written communication; thinking skills, including analysis, synthesis, and evaluation; group skills such as cooperation and appreciation

Materials: reference materials, including sets of encyclopedias, books, and videos about ancient Rome; copies of pages 58–61; writing materials

Procedure: Start the activity in a whole-class group. Explain to the students that they are going to make up their own game similar to television's Jeopardy. Demonstrate how the game is played. Then, as a class, brainstorm categories that pertain to ancient Rome for your own game (suggestions: roads, aqueducts, rulers, clothes, wars, buildings, entertainment, empires, locations, language). Write the categories on the board and have the students go to their groups.

Distribute pages 58–61 to each group. Each group can then choose five categories and write them on their "Category Strips." These will be pinned to the bulletin board or taped to the chalkboard when the group has its turn. The groups can use reference materials to determine five answers and questions for each of their categories. The answers can be written on the "Answer/Dollar Amount Strips" (with the dollar amount on one side and the answer on the other). These strips will be displayed below the "Category Strips" with the dollar amount facing the audience. The questions can be written on the "Question Cards" with a notation for the corresponding category and dollar amount.

When these preparations are complete, the whole class can come back together. Each group will lead its own part of the game. The students will raise their hands and wait to be called on. The group earns the strip with the answer on it when a member of that group scores. The group with the highest total dollar amount at the end of the game wins.

To Simplify: Create the game from material you are studying and play it as a whole group.

To Expand: Have students create answers and questions for Double Jeopardy. Preparations for this can be done as homework, and the game can be played at school on the following day.

Evaluation: Evaluate cooperative learning skills by observing students as they work in their groups. Evaluate knowledge and recall of information while the game is being played. Make appropriate notes on the anecdotal record forms (page 26), which can later be added to the students' portfolios.

Processing: Process with the whole class by having the students discuss the game. What did they like best? Least? What was easiest? Hardest? What might they do differently the next time?

The Past   *Ancient Rome*

Category Strips

Write the names of the five categories chosen by your group on these strips. You will need two of these sheets.

Ancient Rome The Past

Answer/Dollar Amount Strips

On one side of each strip below, write one of these dollar amounts: $100, $200, $300, $400, and $500. After you have written your questions and answers, write the answers on the other sides of the strips. (The questions will go on cards.) Arrange the strips so that the answer for the easiest question is on the $100 strip and the rest get progressively more difficult, up to the $500 strip.

©1995 Teacher Created Materials, Inc. #651 Cooperative Learning Activities for Language Arts

The Past   Ancient Rome

Question Cards

Write your questions on these question cards. Be sure to add the information about category and dollar amount.

Question: Category: _____ Dollar Amount: _____	**Question:** Category: _____ Dollar Amount: _____
Question: Category: _____ Dollar Amount: _____	**Question:** Category: _____ Dollar Amount: _____
Question: Category: _____ Dollar Amount: _____	**Question:** Category: _____ Dollar Amount: _____

#651 Cooperative Learning Activities for Language Arts   ©1995 Teacher Created Materials, Inc.

Ancient Rome   The Past

Game Directions and Diagram

Directions:

When each group takes its turn, the category strips are taped or pinned to a bulletin board over the matching answer and dollar amount strips. The group's spokesperson starts at one side of the room and questions the groups in order. The dialogue will go something like this:

Spokesperson: "Who wants to be first in group x?" (The spokesperson calls on a player who raises his/her hand.)

Player: "I'll take (category) for (dollar amount)." (Example: "I'll take 'Empire' for $100.")

The spokesperson takes down the $100 strip under "Empire" and reads the answer written on the back. If the player gives the correct question, as verified by the question card, the spokesperson hands the player the strip. The strip amount is added to the score of the player's group.

Play continues until all answers and questions are used. The group with the highest score wins.

Diagram:

$100	$100	$100	$100	$100
$200	$200	$200	$200	$200
$300	$300	$300	$300	$300
$400	$400	$400	$400	$400
$500	$500	$500	$500	$500

©1995 Teacher Created Materials, Inc.   #651 Cooperative Learning Activities for Language Arts

The Past

Middle Ages

> **Purpose:** to build a specialized vocabulary for the study of the Middle Ages; to continue the process of developing cooperative learning skills
>
> **Skills:** basic research and dictionary skills, including the ability to use alphabetical order; reading and listening comprehension; oral and written communication; thinking skills, including analysis, synthesis, and evaluation; group skills such as cooperation, appreciation, and the ability to reach consensus
>
> **Materials:** copies of pages 63–65; reference materials, including sets of encyclopedias, dictionaries, and other relevant books; writing materials

Procedure: Start the activity in a whole-class group. Tell students they will be moving on in time to the Middle Ages. They will be working in groups to complete a wordsearch and a worksheet dealing with words that are important for the study of that time period. They will be looking up words and general information, writing down their ideas, and then comparing the results and reaching consensus on the best way to define the words. Tell students they will know they have reached consensus when everybody agrees with a decision.

Distribute page 63 to each student and place a stack of "Definition Worksheets" (pages 64 and 65) on each group's table. Have students read the directions on the worksheets, decide what to do first, and agree on roles within the group. Walk around the room to give help and answer questions.

When complete, have each group share their definitions with the class. Collect the completed, agreed upon list of definitions from each group. Make enough copies for each member of the group to keep one in his or her notebook for future reference.

To Simplify: Discuss the words and their meanings as a whole-class group. Have the students complete the wordsearch in their groups.

To Expand: For homework, give students graph paper and have them create their own wordsearches. Instead of collecting this homework, have students exchange papers and attempt to solve one another's wordsearches.

Evaluation: Evaluate the products produced by the groups when they share their definitions with the large group. Evaluate the way in which students reach consensus by observing them as they work in their groups. Make appropriate notes on the anecdotal record forms (page 26), which can later be added to the students' portfolios.

Processing: Process with the whole class by having the students discuss the degree of ease or difficulty with which they reached consensus. How did they decide on the best way to define a word? What criteria did they use? Which was easier—writing the definitions or working the puzzle? Why?

Middle Ages

The Past

Name_____

Middle Ages Wordsearch

Find the words in the word bank in the wordsearch puzzle below.

Word Bank

postern gate	feudalism	knight	homage
moat	lord	page	vassal
gatehouse	drawbridge	chivalry	duel
chapel	battlements	serf	ramparts
donjon	excommunication	clergy	interdict
keep	portcullis	nobles	Crusades

```
Q M W C H A P E L E K R C D V A S S A L R T
P O S T E R N G A T E Y L O R D T R U I O P
O A A D U E L A S D E Y E N F R N A G H T C
R T K L Z X C T V B P R R J N A E M M N C R
T V T C P A G E X Z L L G O K W M P J H I U
C F H D S A P H O I U A Y N Y B E A T R D S
U W G S E L B O N Q W V E R T R L R Y U R A
L O I P A F E U D A L I S M S M S I T T D F E D
L H N J K L Z S X C V H B N M D T S Q W T E
I R K T Y U S E R F I C O P L G A J G D N S
S W C H O V R L R Y Q U E R T E B A D G I J
E X C O M M U N I C A T I O N H O M A G E F
```

©1995 Teacher Created Materials, Inc.   63   #651 Cooperative Learning Activities for Language Arts

The Past   *Middle Ages*

Name_____

Definitions Worksheet

Using the same word bank used for the wordsearch, arrange the words in alphabetical order and write them on the numbered lines below. (You will find the word bank at the bottom of the next page.) Write the definition of each word. If there is more than one definition for a word, use the definition that best applies to the Middle Ages. When everyone in your group has completed this part of the activity, compare your definitions. When you have all agreed on the best definitions, copy them on a new worksheet and be ready to share your work with the large group.

1. _____

2. _____

3. _____

4. _____

5. _____

6. _____

7. _____

8. _____

9. _____

10. _____

11. _____

12. _____

Middle Ages *The Past*

Definitions Worksheet (cont.)

13. _____

14. _____

15. _____

16. _____

17. _____

18. _____

19. _____

20. _____

21. _____

22. _____

23. _____

24. _____

Word Bank

postern gate	feudalism	knight	homage
moat	lord	page	vassal
gatehouse	drawbridge	chivalry	duel
chapel	battlements	serf	ramparts
donjon	excommunication	clergy	interdict
keep	portcullis	nobles	Crusades

The Past

Explorers

Purpose: to practice using research skills in preparing a report, both oral and written; to further develop group skills; to learn about explorers

Skills: basic research skills, including notetaking from various sources; reading and listening comprehension; oral and written communication; thinking skills, including analysis, synthesis, and evaluation; group skills such as cooperation, appreciation, and the ability to reach consensus

Materials: a copy of pages 67 and 68 for each group; a copy of page 69 for each student; an enlarged copy of pages 67 and 68 to be posted on the classroom wall where students can reach it; reference materials, including sets of encyclopedias and other relevant books; writing materials; fine-line colored markers (a different color per group)

Procedure: This activity will take at least one week to complete. Start the activity in a whole-class group. Tell the students they will be moving on in time to the Age of Exploration and you will be assigning each group the name of an explorer. They will be working in their groups to research and prepare written reports about their explorers. They will plan interesting ways to present their reports orally to the class. The reports will show the routes their explorer followed. These routes can be drawn on their small maps and be ready for drawing on the big class map.

Place a stack of maps (pages 67 and 68) on each group's table. Prepare students to discuss in their groups the things that need to be done and make a list. You might want to write a suggested list on the board. For example:

1. Written report   a. What sections will we have?   b. Who wants to be responsible for each section?
2. Oral report   a. How do we create an interesting presentation? Write down our ideas.
                       b. Choose a presentation plan.
3. Map route   a. Who should do it? One person? All of us?   b. What will we use to find the route?

When students go to their groups, walk around to answer questions and give any necessary help. Show one group at a time how to take notes as they read. Use "Forms for Notes" on page 69.

When complete, have the students present their reports. Collect the reports to read at your leisure. Be sure to keep them for an Open House display.

To Simplify: With the whole group, model the process for taking notes from reading materials. Have each student take notes from a book while you give individual help.

To Expand: Students who have extra time can determine the dimensions of their explorer's ship. They can measure and draw the ship with chalk on the blacktop. If they also find out how many people sailed on the ship, that number of students can be invited to stand on "deck."

Evaluation: Evaluate the reports according to the following points: good information, interesting presentation, and the ability to transfer the explorers' routes from the small maps to the large map. Make appropriate notes on the anecdotal record forms (page 26), which can later be added to the students' portfolios.

Processing: Process with the whole class by having the students discuss the process they used to write a group report. How did they decide on who would do each job? Which was easier—writing the report or deciding on the jobs? Why?

#651 Cooperative Learning Activities for Language Arts   ©1995 Teacher Created Materials, Inc.

Explorers   *The Past*

Group Name _____

Group Members _____

_____

Outline Map of the World

Write your explorer's name below and draw his/her route or routes on the map.

Our explorer is _____.

©1995 Teacher Created Materials, Inc.   #651 Cooperative Learning Activities for Language Arts

The Past   *Explorers*

Outline Map of the World (cont.)

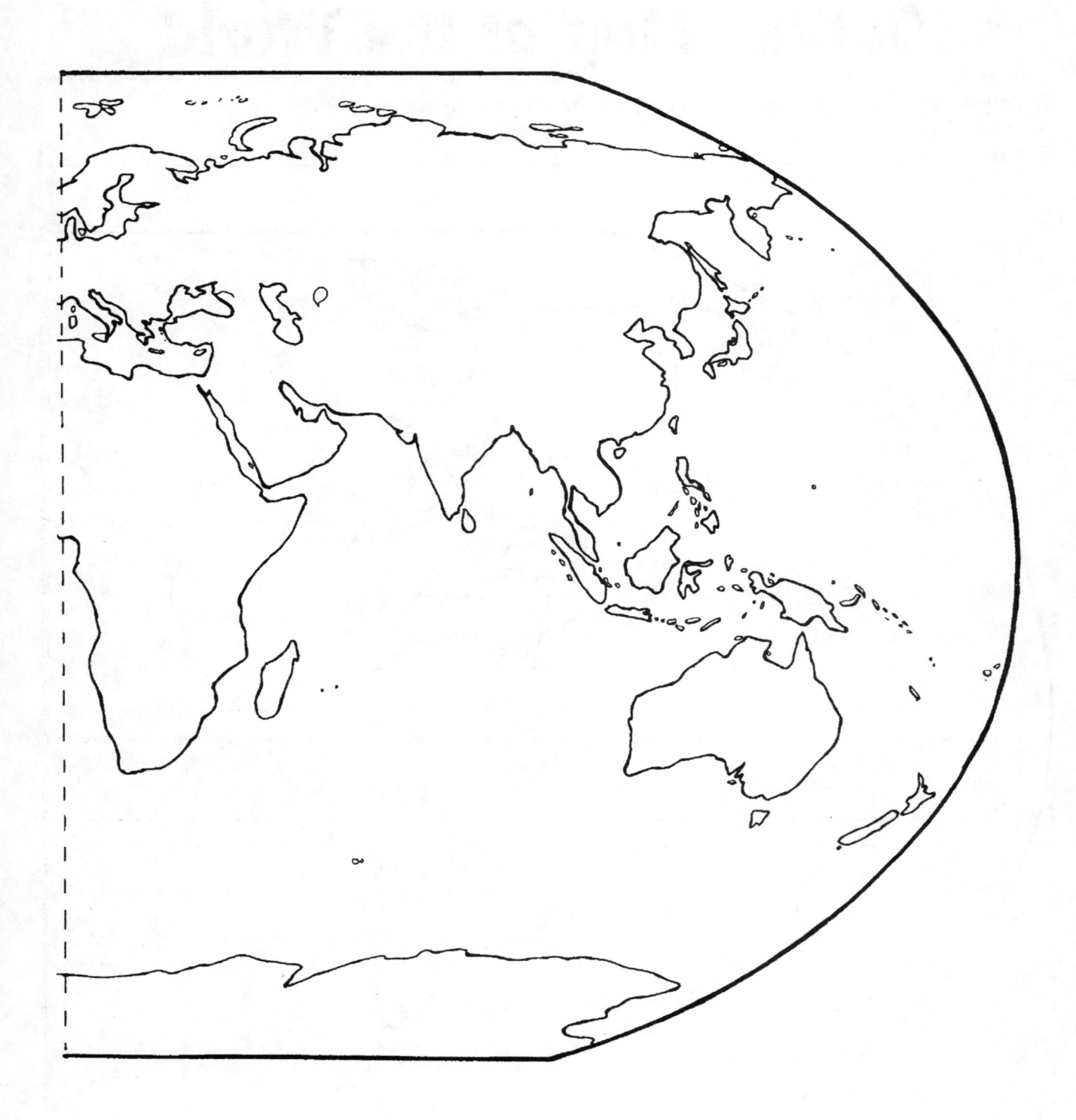

Explorers *The Past*

Name_____

Forms for Notes

Fill out one of these forms every time you read a book about your explorer. You will never again need to wonder where you found your information.

The book I am reading is _____
by _____

Page #	Note

The book I am reading is _____
by _____

Page #	Note

The book I am reading is _____
by _____

Page #	Note

The book I am reading is _____
by _____

Page #	Note

The book I am reading is _____
by _____

Page #	Note

©1995 Teacher Created Materials, Inc. #651 Cooperative Learning Activities for Language Arts

The Present

"The History of Time Travel" Play

> **Purpose:** to create and script a time-travel adventure to a destination of choice
>
> **Skills:** written and oral language; acting; organization; teamwork; creativity
>
> **Materials:** time machine (page 14); copies of pages 86 and 87; reference books, including encyclopedias; access to a library; art supplies; costume supplies

Procedure: In this activity, student groups plan, write, and present a time-travel play. Have students refer to page 86, "Elements of Theater." Then, begin the activity by holding a whole-class discussion about plays. You may wish to have the children read a play in class, letting the students "play" the parts in an oral reading. Then, explain to students that they will be writing a play about a time-travel adventure.

The students will use the class time machine as part of their sets, and they should incorporate it into their plays. Give them sufficient class time to write and edit their plays. After they are written, work with individual groups to discuss casting and rehearsal. Give the children plenty of time to practice their plays.

After the students feel they are ready, let them have a dress rehearsal for you. Teachers can work with each team's director to help them iron out any production "bugs." After the students feel comfortable, let them present their plays for the other groups on a special "Play Day."

To Simplify: Have students write a time-travel play and present it in an oral reading, using their scripts.

To Expand: Have ambitious students present their plays at a school assembly or for different classes.

Evaluate: Work with student groups at the various stages of this activity to make several evaluations. Use the anecdotal record form on page 26 to note individual student performances. Add this form to each child's portfolio.

Processing: Give the children time to critique their own plays. Ask the children to take a supportive and complimentary attitude with the other teams, looking for what they liked in one another's plays.

The Present

Clocks

Purpose: to research and study the history of clocks; to build and display actual clocks and place them in a clock museum

Skills: critical thinking; logic; analysis; cooperation; organization; research; planning

Materials: art supplies such as clay, paints, and glue; paper plates; toothpicks; copies of pages 72–78; a display area in the classroom for a clock museum; index cards; additional materials as determined by the exact nature of the clock to be built

Procedure: In this activity, student teams will research, plan, and build working clocks. Begin with a whole-class discussion about clocks. Give the student teams several days or class periods to research information. Provide reference books, including encyclopedias, or have student teams visit the school or neighborhood library. After teams have compiled as much information as possible about clocks, ask them to begin planning their own clock, using pages 72–78. Spend time assisting each group and hearing about their plans and what materials they will need.

At the next team-meeting time, have the students assemble their clocks. Give them the opportunity to test their clocks. (For example, children making sundials will have to go outside.) Next, have the class come together. Student representatives from each team can demonstrate the team's clock.

Next, have the student teams return to their groups to write a description of their clock for the clock museum. Ask the students to bring clocks and watches from home, on loan, to add to the clock museum, as well. This museum provides an interesting and decorative display for Open House.

To Simplify: Demonstrate the concept of a sundial, using a stick in the ground. Have the student teams make a simple sundial using paper plates or simply have them gather or make models of clocks for the clock museum.

To Expand: Have students make a "time" video. Videotape members of each team displaying and explaining their clock. Have members of each team work together to write and narrate the video.

Evaluation: Evaluate individual students by using the anecdotal record form on page 26. Add the form to each student's portfolio. Interact with the student groups to discern further information about each student's participation.

Processing: Process with your whole class by observing them preparing the display for the clock museum. Give the students time to look at each other's clocks and discuss the creation process. Let students share how they felt about the activity, what was difficult, and what they would do differently the next time.

The Present *Clocks*

Clock Project Planning Form

Team Name _____

Team Members_____
_____
_____

List members who will be responsible for these tasks:

- **Brainstormers** _____
- **Inventors**_____
- **Craftspersons** _____
- **Writers** _____
- **Spokesperson** _____

Your team will be building an actual clock. Begin by finding out as much about clocks as possible. Use your library for reference materials. Then, decide what kind of clock you will build. Use your "How to Build a Clock" information sheets to help you decide which kind of clock you will build.

Make a sketch of how your clock will look.

Sketch

List the materials you will need:
_____
_____
_____
_____

Clocks *The Present*

Clock Project Completion Form

Team Name _____

Team Members _____

_____

_____

As a group, complete the following questions and descriptions.

1. What kind of clock did your team make?
   _____
   _____

2. How did you make it?
   _____
   _____

3. Does it keep accurate time?
   _____
   _____

4. What was the most difficult thing about making your clock?
   _____
   _____

Use this space to describe your clock and how it works. Later, copy this information onto an index card for your clock museum.

The Present   **Clocks**

Activity Brainstorm Form

Team Name _____

Team Members _____

_____

Purpose of Brainstorm _____

_____

Ideas

Clocks   *The Present*

How to Build a Clock

What time is it? Look at a clock. Measuring time has been important to civilizations for thousands of years. However, the way we measure time has changed. Today, we use electric outlets, batteries, or sometimes even atomic energy to power our clocks. Older clocks are often wound. These clocks have hairsprings that are wound tight to make the small wheels inside the clock move. But long, long ago, people used the sun, water, sand, or candles to tell time.

Building a working model of an ancient clock is fun and easy. Use the following instructions to help your team build a model of an ancient clock for your clock museum.

Sundials

Sundials are the most ancient way of telling time. As the sun moves from morning to night, its passage can be measured in hours.

Early civilizations used their sundials to measure the length of an hour. With that knowledge, they were able to make other kinds of clocks with sand, water, and candles.

To make a simple sundial, you will need the following supplies:

- paper plate with a 10" (25 cm) diameter
- index paper
- scissors
- glue
- compass

Make a slanted blade by cutting a triangle from a piece of index paper. (See the measurements below.) Make a 1" (2.5 cm) fold at the base of the triangle as shown in the diagram. Glue the triangle to the paper-plate base. (See the illustration.) Next, place your sundial outside so that the triangle is aligned with north and south.

Mark off the positions of the shadow as it appears every hour from sunrise to sunset. To do so, follow the directions on page 76.

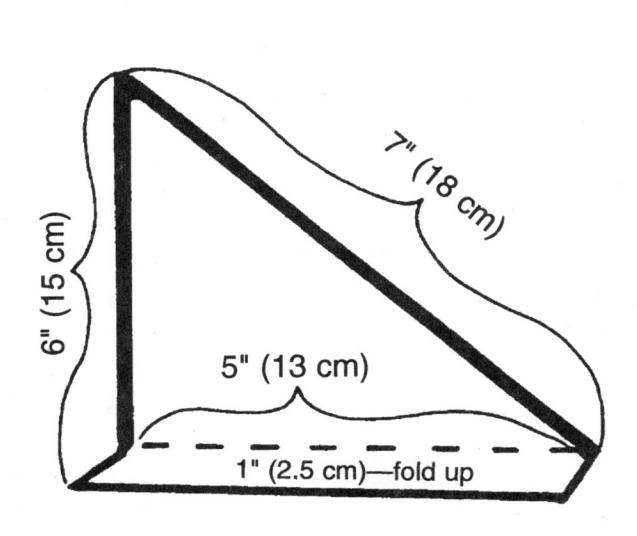

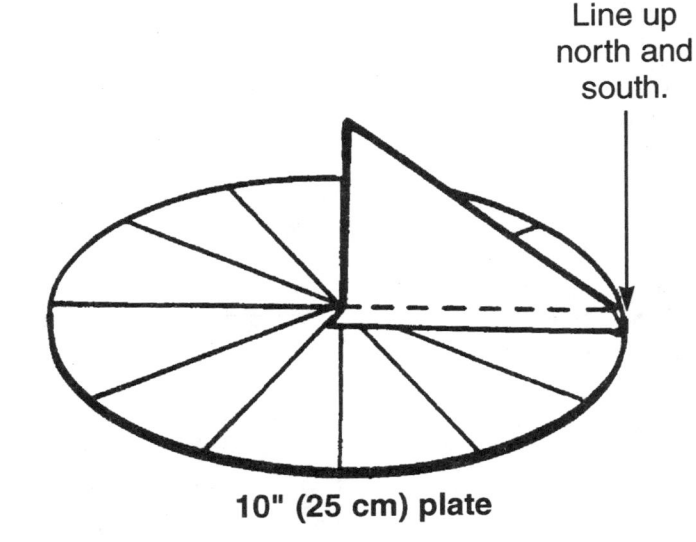

The Present   **Clocks**

How to Build a Clock (cont.)

Sundial—Record and Write

As a group, observe the shadow on the sundial at various times during the day. Record your observations by drawing the shadows and times on the sundials below. Write what you were doing at these times (for example, outdoor recess, lunch, or a classroom activity).

○ _____   ○ _____
   Activity   Activity

_____   _____
_____   _____
_____   _____

○ _____   ○ _____
   Activity   Activity

_____   _____
_____   _____
_____   _____

○ _____   ○ _____
   Activity   Activity

_____   _____
_____   _____
_____   _____

Clocks   *The Present*

How to Build a Clock (cont.)

Candle Clocks

Candle clocks are easy and fun to make. To make a candle clock, you will need the following supplies.

- two long candles
- two candle holders
- matches (to be used only with adult supervision)

To make a candle clock, you will time one candle as it burns and mark the other candle to show the hours as they pass. Ancient people used a sundial to do this. You will probably want to use a modern clock.

Stand the candles next to each other. With adult help and/or supervision, light one of them. After an hour, blow out the burning candle and make a mark on the unlit candle to show how far the lighted candle burned in an hour. Mark the rest of the candle in the same way.

You may want to try different kinds of candles, because some will burn quickly and some will not. Make notes about your clock as you construct it. Then, be sure to make an extra example for your clock museum.

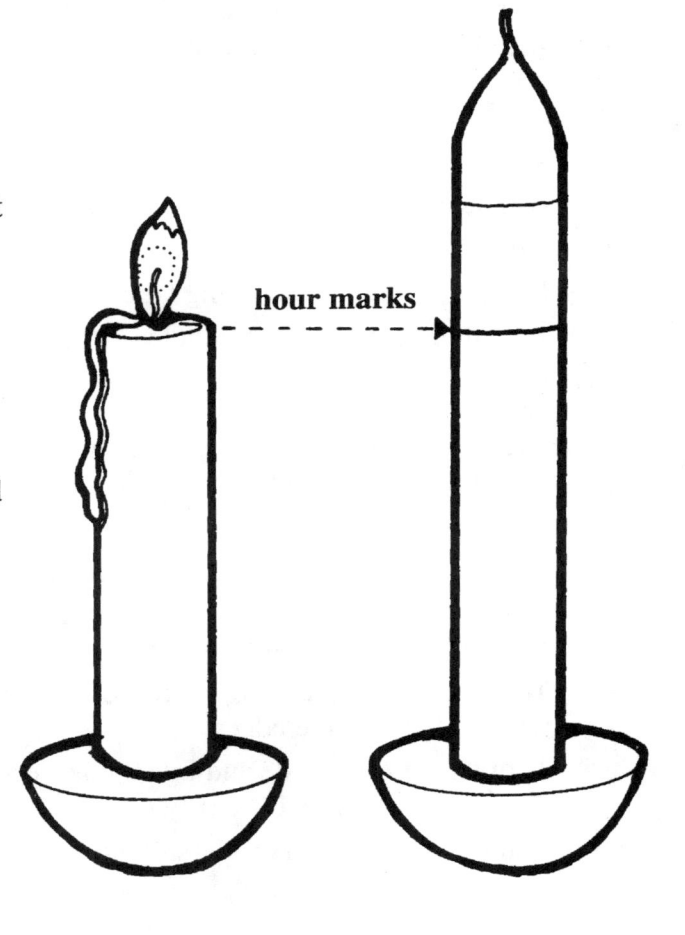

Notes: _____

_____

_____

_____

_____

_____

_____

_____

_____

©1995 Teacher Created Materials, Inc.   77   #651 Cooperative Learning Activities for Language Arts

The Present   *Clocks*

How to Build a Clock (cont.)

Sand Clocks

Many people are familiar with sand clocks. Often, they are called egg timers. Sometimes small sand clocks are included with board games, and anyone who has seen *The Wizard of Oz* will likely remember the sand clock used by the wicked witch when she held Dorothy captive.

To make a sand clock, you will need the following supplies:

- sand
- two large mayonnaise jars or plastic bottles with wide mouths
- a piece of cardboard
- heavy tape (duct or masking tape)
- something to poke a small hole
- scissors

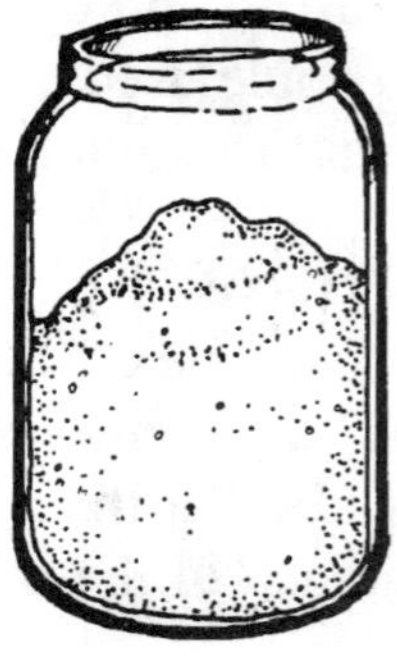

To decide how much sand is needed to make your clock, practice a few times. Here is what you will do:

1. Put sand in one jar.
2. Cut a piece of cardboard to fit on the top of the jar.
3. Poke a hole in the center of the cardboard large enough for sand to pass through one tiny bit at a time.
4. Tape the cardboard on top of the jar carefully so no sand will fall through the edges.
5. Turn the jar on its side and line up the second jar. Tape the edges together with sturdy tape.
6. Carefully turn the jars right-side-up so that the jar with the sand in it is on the top.
7. Time how quickly the sand passes through into the bottom jar.
8. Mark the bottom jar with the time that has passed.

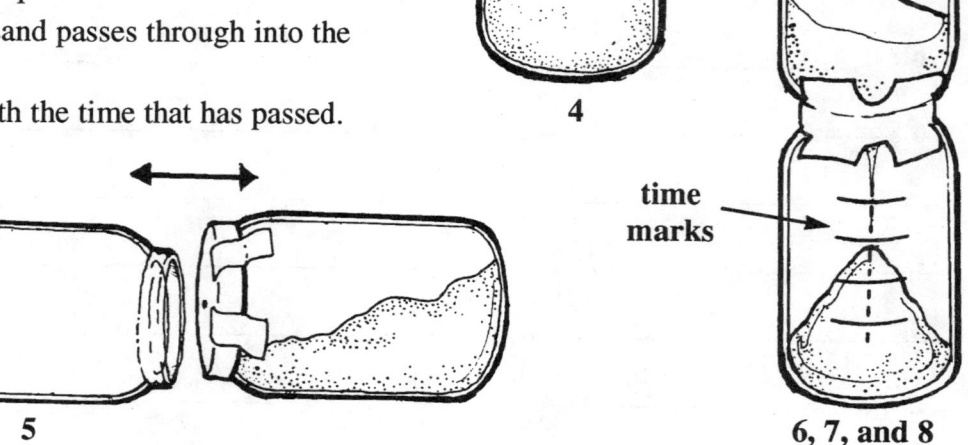

Water Clocks

A water clock is like a sand clock. The idea is to let water drip from one container to another through a small hole and measure how long it takes. Read the directions for the sand clock and see if you can plan a way to make a water clock. Be sure to get help and permission from your teacher before you start to build a water clock.

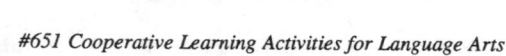

The Present

Dictionary of Time

Purpose: to create a classroom dictionary of time, defining commonly used "time" phrases, words, and slang

Skills: research; brainstorming; reading; writing; consensus; decision-making; critical thinking

Materials: copies of pages 80–83; reference books about time, including encyclopedias; art and writing supplies; one regular class dictionary per student or pair of students

Procedure: Begin the activity by holding a whole-class discussion about dictionaries and their usefulness. Have students explain how to look up a word, alphabetical order, and the meaning of *definition*.

Next, discuss the meanings of *slang* and *phrase*. Explain common phrases or sayings by giving some examples. Then, have the students work in groups, using their brainstorming sheets, to think of as many words, phrases, and slang terms about time as they can.

After they have completed this, the group should discuss among themselves possible definitions for their terms. Next, selected members of the group should use reference texts to verify their ideas.

After student groups have completed the research for their dictionaries, they can make rough drafts, using reprints of page 82. After they have proofed and edited their work, students should make final copies for a classroom dictionary of time.

Finally, have each group decide upon an idea for the cover of the dictionary and submit this idea to the whole class via a group spokesperson. Take a vote to decide which cover design will be chosen. Also vote on which group or members from each group will create the cover.

To Simplify: Omit the publishing step and have the student groups simply brainstorm and define their time terms.

To Expand: Have student groups create an audio dictionary. Use a tape recorder for students to make a book on tape. Display it with the time dictionary at Open House. You might also hold a contest to determine the student group that can think of the most additional, unrecorded phrases.

Evaluation: Evaluate this activity by working with individual student groups and examining their brainstorming worksheets and published results. Use the anecdotal record form (page 26) to make notes for individual student portfolios.

Processing: Process with the whole class by having students take turns looking up words and phrases and discussing them with the class. Refer to the dictionary whenever appropriate.

The Present   *Dictionary of Time*

Time Dictionary

Your group will be helping to make a time dictionary. You will need to brainstorm to think of words, phrases, and slang that have something to do with time. Below, you will find a few examples.

Words:	**Phrases:**	**Slang:**
time	hurry up	jam
clock	too late	move it
minute	better late than never	

Choose members of your group to do each of the following jobs:

- brainstormers
- researchers
- writers
- editors

The brainstormers for our group are:

_____   _____
_____   _____
_____   _____

The researchers for our group are:

_____   _____
_____   _____

The writers for our group are:

_____   _____
_____   _____

The editors for our group are:

_____   _____
_____   _____

After you have completed this part of the activity, begin to write your dictionary rough draft, using the "Dictionary Page" (page 82).

#651 Cooperative Learning Activities for Language Arts   80   ©1995 Teacher Created Materials, Inc.

Dictionary of Time **The Present**

Time Brainstorming Worksheet

The Present   *Dictionary of Time*

Dictionary Page

Dictionary of Time **The Present**

Our Time Dictionary

written by

_____

_____
_____
_____
_____
_____
_____
_____

©1995 Teacher Created Materials, Inc. 83 #651 *Cooperative Learning Activities for Language Arts*

The Present

Time Out for Role Plays

Purpose: to invent and script short role-plays, using as many words, phrases, and slang terms from the time dictionary as possible

Skills: imagination; teamwork; decision-making; reaching consensus; reading, writing, and oral language skills; drama and communication skills

Materials: time dictionary (page 79); copies of pages 85–87; costumes; props; art materials

Procedure: In this activity, the students use the time dictionary they created in the previous activity to invent and script their own role-plays. You may wish to have students write mini-plays and take several weeks to produce them, or you may wish to ask the children to spend one class period putting together a role-play, and then have student teams present their role-plays to the class immediately thereafter.

Begin this activity by reading a short play selection. (You may also wish to use this activity to complement lessons about plays and playwrights.) Have the students look at "Elements of Theater" (page 86) and discuss this with the members of their group. Then, explain to the whole class that they will be preparing a role-play or mini-play to present to the rest of the class. Their objective in preparing their presentation and script is to use as many "time" phrases as possible in their play while still making sense.

They will need to agree upon a story idea, write a script, and decide who will play the parts. After team presentations are ready, have the students present their plays one at a time to the rest of the class. Have the students count the time words and phrases to determine who has the most. Award the winning team, if possible, with inexpensive digital quartz watches or simply with candy or another treat.

To Simplify: Have the students spend fifteen minutes writing a short role-play. In "improv" fashion, have students create as they go, using as many time words and phrases as they can remember.

To Expand: Have students make costumes, rehearse, and build sets for their plays. Audio or videotape the results or have teams go from room to room to present their plays for other classes.

Evaluation: Evaluate individuals during the preparation period of the activity by going from group to group to interact. Evaluate again by viewing student participation in their presentations.

Processing: The processing step can be the actual play presentation and the follow-up discussion. Have the children decide which team wins (has the most time words) and award prizes.

Time Out for Role-Plays   **The Present**

Play Worksheet

Team Name _____

Team Members _____
_____

Your team will be writing a mini-play. Your play may be about anything, but you must use as many words, phrases, and slang phrases as possible from the time dictionary you created earlier. In your teams, decide who will perform each of the following jobs:

- brainstormers
- writers
- director
- actors

Here is a list of things you will need to do.

1. Brainstorm ideas for your play.
2. Refer to the time dictionary for time words.
3. Write a rough draft of your play.
4. Edit, correct, and write a published copy.
5. Decide who will play what parts.
6. Practice your play.
7. Decide whether or not your team will use props and costumes.
8. Practice some more!
9. Present your play for the rest of the class.

The name of our play is_____

Our play is about _____
_____
_____

Cast of Characters

Character	**Played by**
_____	_____
_____	_____
_____	_____
_____	_____

Notes _____
_____
_____

Elements of Theater

Below is a mini-guide to plays. Read this page carefully with your group before you begin to write your play. This information will help you to be aware of everything you need to produce a play. Curtain up!

The Play: A play is a story that is written to be presented orally by actors to an audience. Actors play the parts of the characters and read dialogue or words as if they are participating in a real, spontaneous conversation. A play is usually presented in a theater; however, sometimes plays are given in makeshift settings like parks or even the street. There are many different kinds of plays. There are dramas, which are serious plays, and comedies, which are meant to be funny. There are also musicals, plays in which the actors not only speak their words but sing them as well.

The Players: Players is another term for actors. Actors are the people who act out the words of the play as if they are really saying the words, not just reading them or reciting them from memory. Actors are chosen or "cast" in a play and given a character to "become." When an actor is cast in a play, he/she receives a copy of the play, a script. He/she reads the words (called "lines") over carefully until they are memorized and can be said without looking at the script. Then, the actor attends rehearsals to learn his/her part with the other actors.

The Dialogue: Dialogue is what the actors say to each other.

Stage Direction: Stage directions are the written instructions in a play that tell the actors what to do while they are saying their lines.

The Set: The set is the stage decoration. Depending on what the play is about, this will vary. A play set in a house will have a set that looks like a house. A play set in an airplane will have a set that looks like an airplane.

The Costumes: Costumes are the clothes that actors wear to make them look like the characters they are playing.

The Props: Props are the objects that actors hold or use to make the action of the play seem real. For example, if two actors are supposed to be drinking tea, they would hold cups and saucers and pretend to be drinking tea. Sometimes, they actually will drink tea to make the play even more authentic.

Rehearsals: Rehearsals are practice times for the actors to learn how to work together and play their parts well.

Director: The director is the person who leads the play. He/she is like a teacher who makes decisions and gives instructions to the actors.

The Performance: The performance is the presentation of the play to the audience.

Time Out for Role-Plays   *The Present*

Script

Act: _____

Scene: _____

Setting: _____

_____ : _____
      (character)   _____
                                                       _____
                                                       _____

_____ : _____
      (character)

_____ : _____
      (character)

_____ : _____
      (character)

Stage directions:

_____
_____
_____

Costume, prop, and set notes:

_____
_____
_____

©1995 Teacher Created Materials, Inc.   #651 Cooperative Learning Activities for Language Arts

The Present

Time Management

> **Purpose:** to learn about time management; to set up group and personal schedules, calendars, and goals
>
> **Skills:** analytical and critical thinking skills; logic; communication; creativity
>
> **Materials:** copies of pages 89–101; one calendar of the current year per group; writing supplies

Procedure: In this activity, students study the idea of time management and apply it to their own lives. Student groups will make a weekly, a monthly, and an annual schedule and set weekly, monthly, and annual goals.

Begin this activity by talking about time management. You may wish to bring examples of schedules or give students the opportunity to view your plan book. Explain that schedules are ways to manage time effectively.

Next, have a class discussion and talk about class schedules involving the different subjects taught daily or weekly and special events like plays or Open House. Then, explain to the teams that they will be making and following team and personal schedules and setting team and personal goals. The students should discuss these ideas in their groups and use the worksheets on pages 89–96. On page 89, the groups will brainstorm their collective schedules. Pages 90 and 91 may be used by each individual as well as by each group. Pages 92–96 may also be used by each individual as well as by each group.

After the students have set their goals and schedules, have a class discussion in which representatives from each group share their process and schedules. Have each group make a copy of its schedule for a master schedule book and have the student groups share their team goals as well. Then, follow up weekly to have students report on their schedules and goals and make needed adjustments.

This activity can continue through an entire year, if desired. Use pages 97–101 for a classroom bulletin board featuring student goal achievement throughout the year. Create a vertical line from pages 98–101. Page 97 will model how to place the triangular tags that also appear on that page. Students can place a tag on the bulletin board when they have completed a goal.

To Simplify: Have students omit the goal step and simply use the schedule pages to make a weekly schedule. Have them follow it for a week.

To Expand: Have student groups meet periodically to discuss their goals and the steps necessary to attain them.

Evaluation: Evaluate this activity by using the anecdotal record form on page 26. Place this form in each student's portfolio. Evaluate individual performances by reviewing the personal goal worksheet that each student completes.

To Process: Start a goal tree. Spray a dead tree or branch gold and have the teams attach colored decorations signifying their achievements. See which team has achieved the most goals. Have a party to celebrate the achievements.

Time Management   *The Present*

Schedule Worksheet

Team Name _____

Team Members _____

_____

_____

Your team will be creating and following team and personal schedules. Use this worksheet to help you get started.

Schedules are for keeping track of what you need to do every day. Some adults use appointment books to keep track of what they need to do daily. In your group, decide what you need to do every day at school and discuss the various things each group member does every day outside of school. Remember to include homework time, meetings, special lessons, sports, or play rehearsals. Use the schedules you create to help you learn to manage your time better.

What We Do at School

What We Do at Home

The Present *Time Management*

Goal Worksheet

Team Name _____
Individual _____

Daily Goals

1. _____
   _____
   _____
2. _____
   _____
   _____
3. _____
   _____
   _____

Weekly Goals

1. _____
   _____
   _____
2. _____
   _____
   _____
3. _____

Yearly Goals

1. _____
   _____
   _____
2. _____
   _____
   _____
3. _____
   _____
   _____

Remember, a goal is something you want to do or achieve on a daily, weekly, or yearly basis. Use the "Goal Tracker Worksheet" (page 91) to keep track of your progress.

#651 Cooperative Learning Activities for Language Arts

Time Management — *The Present*

Goal Tracker Worksheet

My Goals:

1. _____
2. _____
3. _____

My plans to meet my goals are:

_____
_____
_____
_____
_____
_____
_____
_____
_____
_____
_____
_____

Met Goals:

1. _____
2. _____
3. _____

What I accomplished:

_____
_____
_____
_____
_____
_____
_____
_____
_____
_____
_____
_____

The Present   *Time Management*

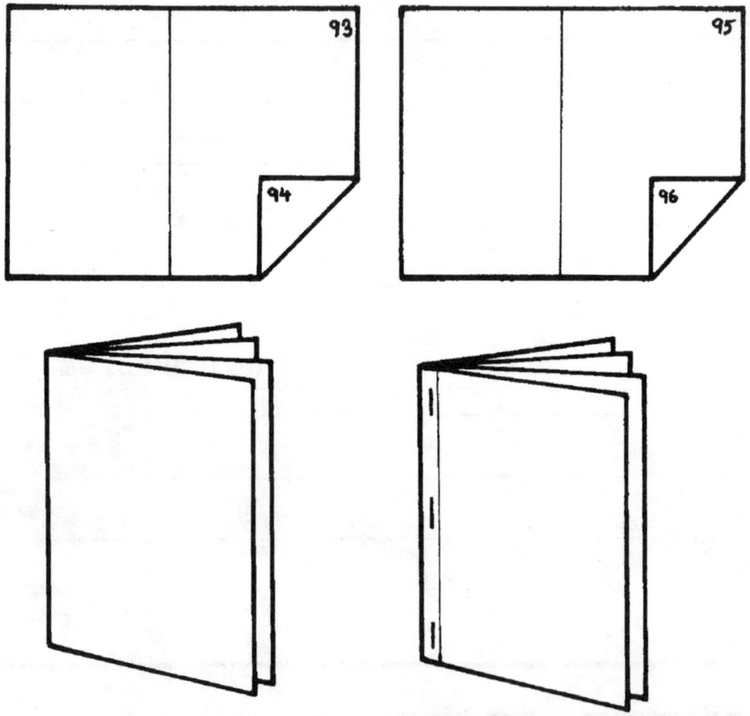

Time Management Scheduler

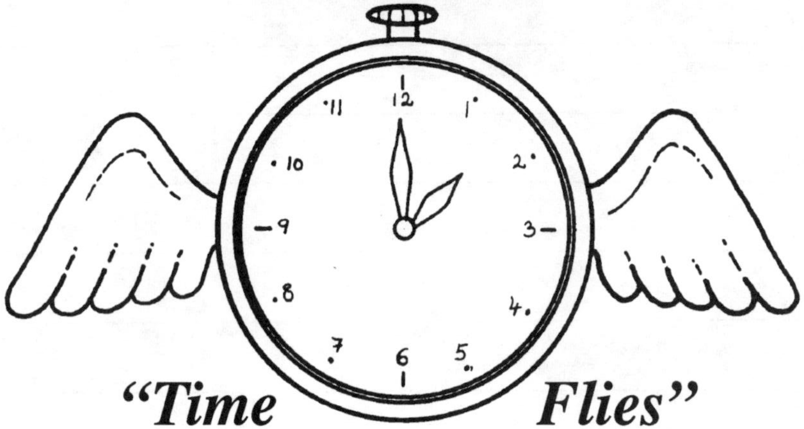

"Time Flies"

Week of _____ to _____

This book belongs to:

Name _____

Room _____

Phone _____

Directions for putting the scheduler together:

1. Duplicate pages 93 and 94 back-to-back.
2. Duplicate pages 95 and 96 back-to-back.
3. Use page 92 as the front and back covers.
4. Stack the other pages in their appropriate order.
5. Fold all pages together.
6. Staple on the side to create a booklet.

#651 Cooperative Learning Activities for Language Arts ©1995 Teacher Created Materials, Inc.

Time Management Scheduler (cont.)

Goal Reminder

Daily
1.
2.
3.

Weekly
1.
2.
3.

Yearly
1.
2.
3.

Notes and Ideas

The Present   *Time Management*

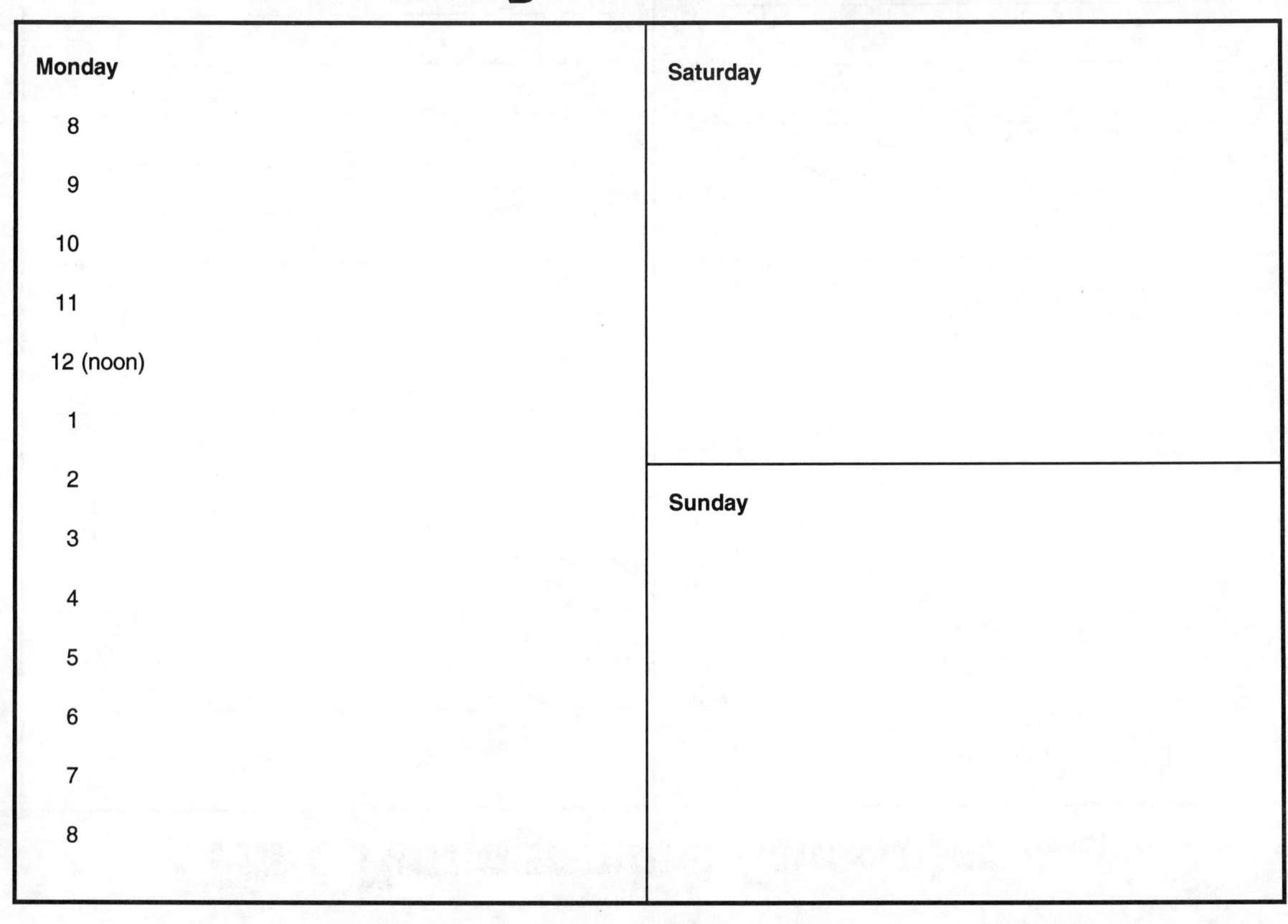

Time Management Scheduler (cont.)

Saturday

Sunday

Monday

8
9
10
11
12 (noon)
1
2
3
4
5
6
7
8

Time Management **The Present**

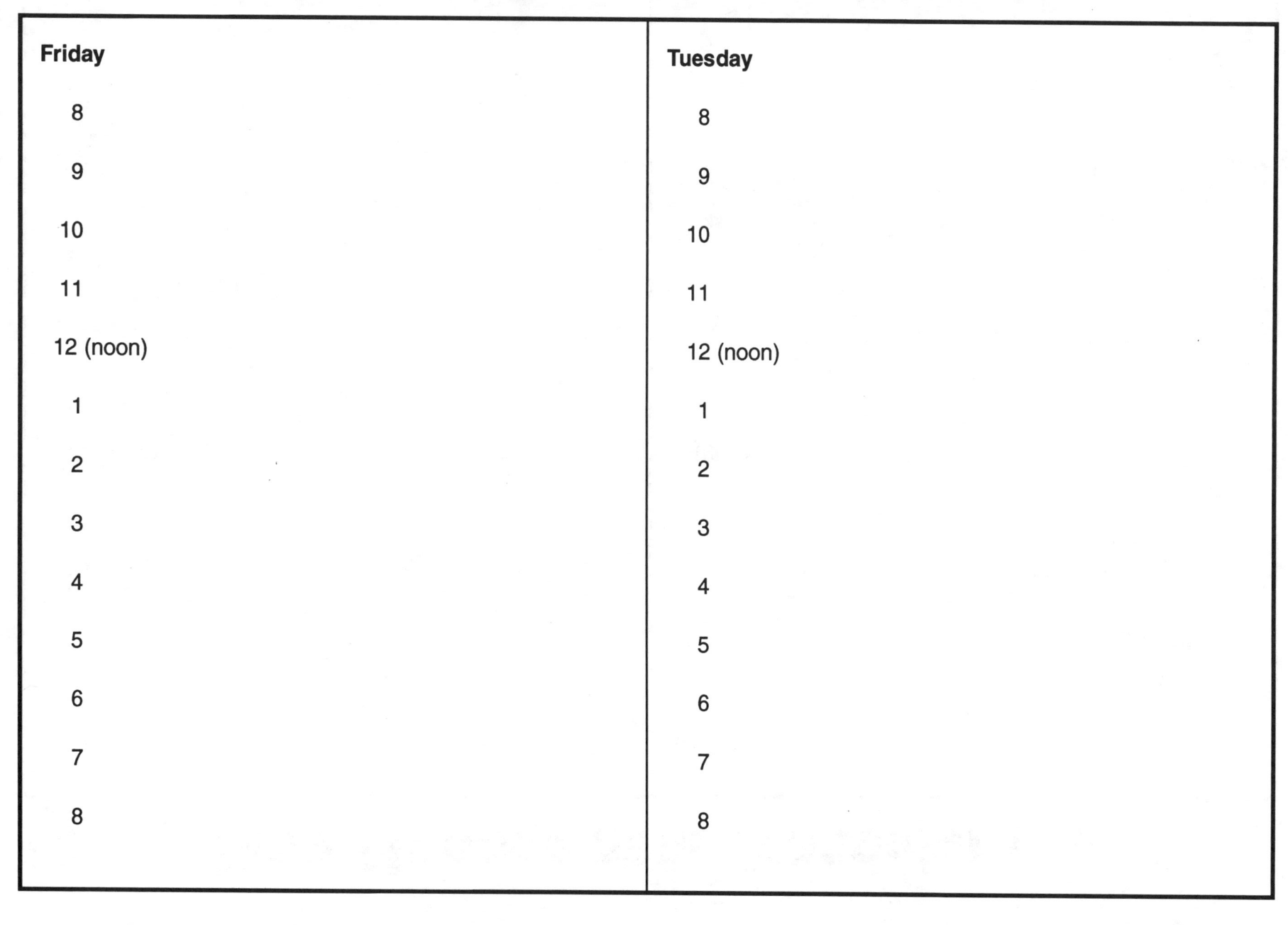

Time Management Scheduler (cont.)

Tuesday
8
9
10
11
12 (noon)
1
2
3
4
5
6
7
8

Friday
8
9
10
11
12 (noon)
1
2
3
4
5
6
7
8

©1995 Teacher Created Materials, Inc. #651 Cooperative Learning Activities for Language Arts

The Present *Time Management*

Time Management Scheduler (cont.)

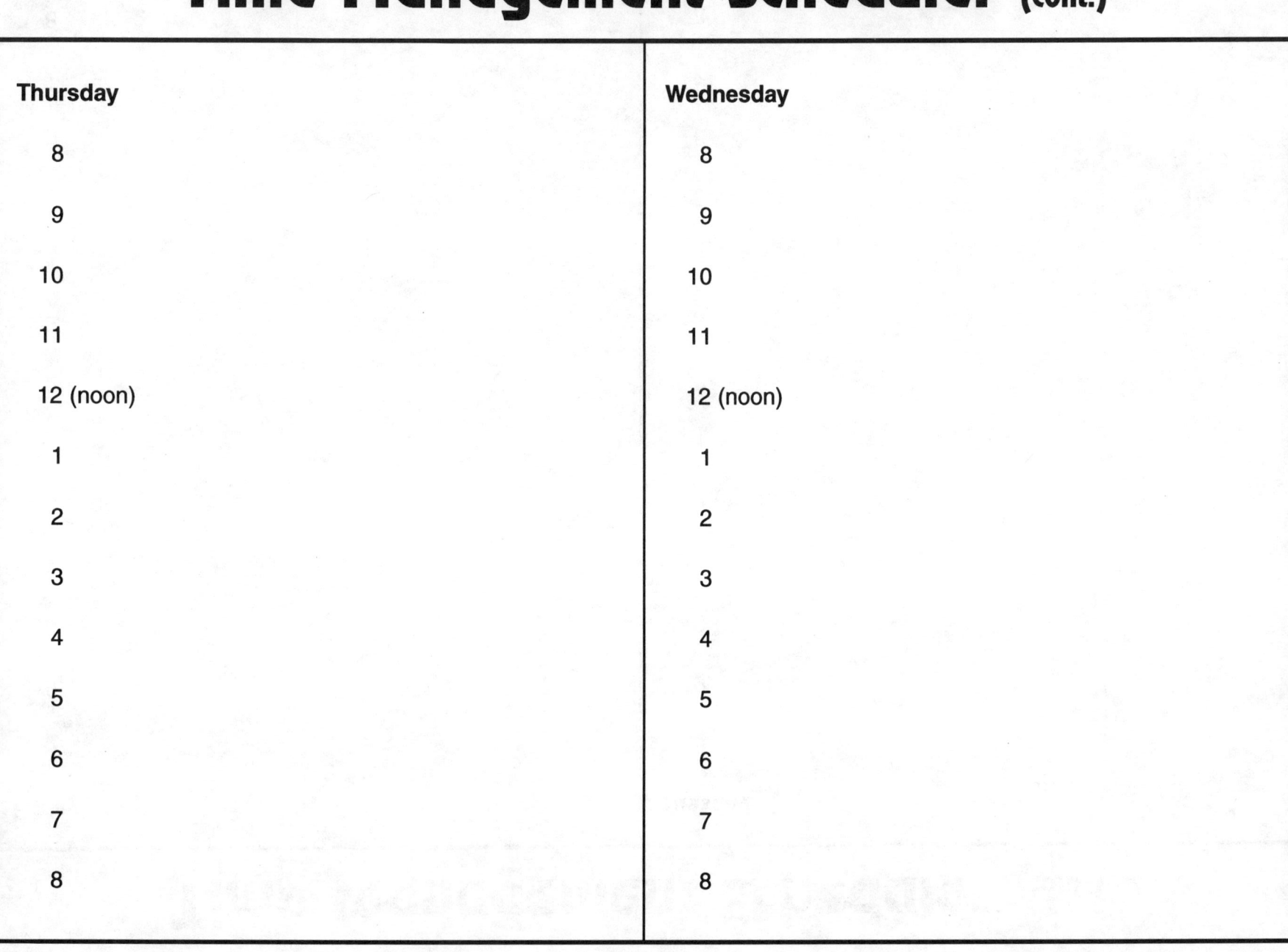

Wednesday

8
9
10
11
12 (noon)
1
2
3
4
5
6
7
8

Thursday

8
9
10
11
12 (noon)
1
2
3
4
5
6
7
8

Time Management   *The Present*

Achievement Flags

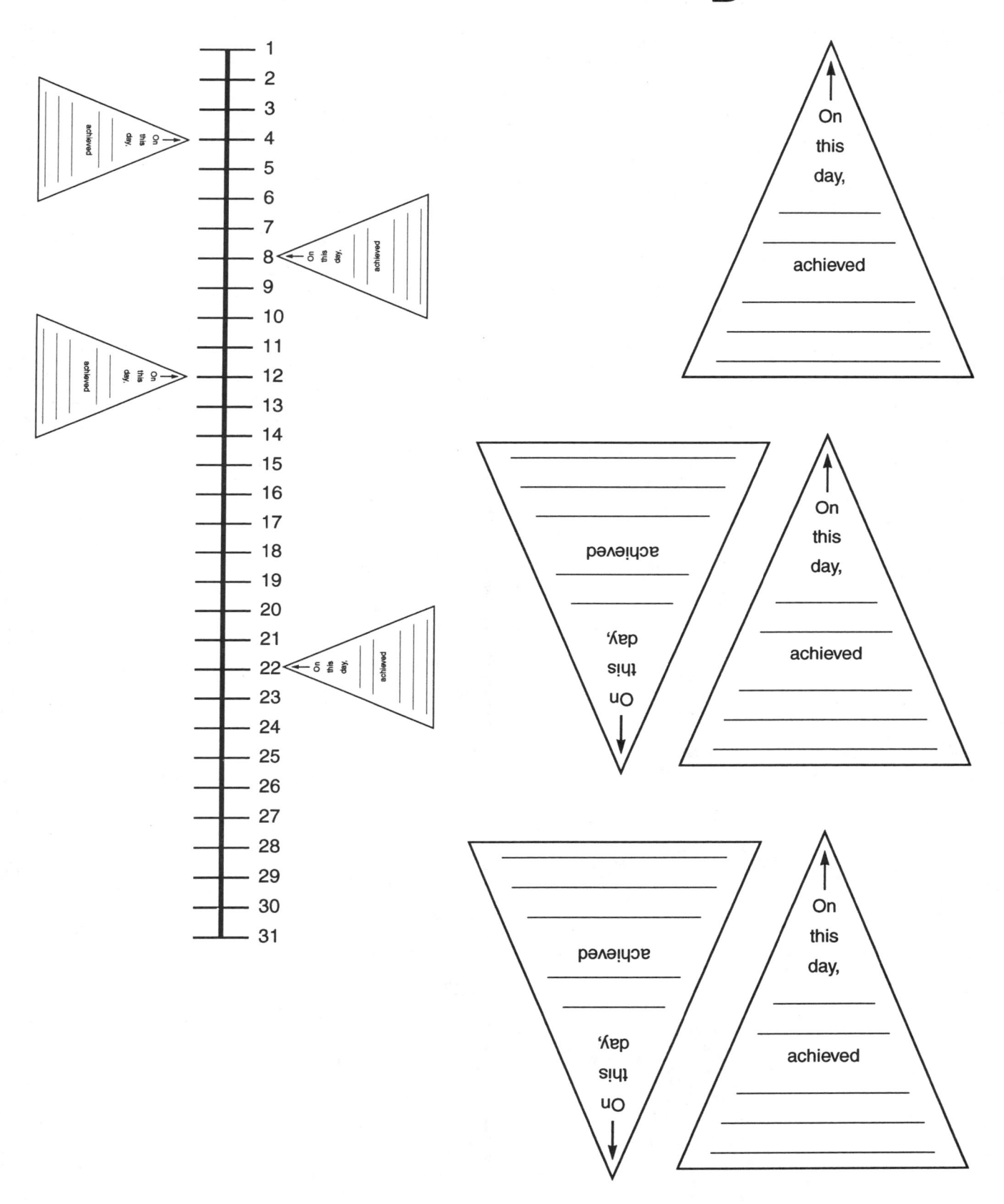

The Present *Time Management*

Twelve-Month Goal Time Line

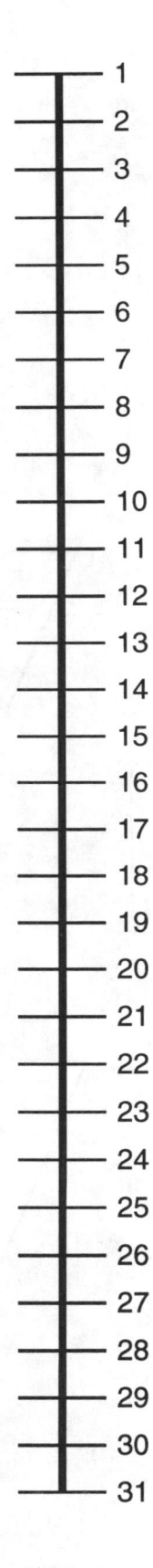

1
2
3
4
5
6
7
8
9
10
11
12
13
14
15
16
17
18
19
20
21
22
23
24
25
26
27
28
29
30
31

Time Management   *The Present*

Twelve-Month Goal Time Line (cont.)

January

February

March

April

The Present   *Time Management*

Twelve-Month Goal Time Line (cont.)

May

June

July

August

Time Management   *The Present*

Twelve-Month Goal Time Line (cont.)

September

October

November

December

The Present

Time of My Life

> **Purpose:** to write and publish biographies
>
> **Skills:** decision-making; interviewing; fact-finding; oral and written language; imagination; creativity; organization; follow-through
>
> **Materials:** copies of pages 103–105; video or audio recording equipment; art supplies; writing supplies

Procedure: The students will work together in groups, reading and discussing biographies of famous people, deciding on their favorites, and, finally, interviewing each other to write and publish class biographies. Begin the activity by holding a class discussion about biographies. You may wish to read selections from famous historical biographies written at the appropriate grade level for your students.

Next, have the class think of famous people of the past or present who are likely to have published biographies about their lives. Write the names mentioned on the board so that students can view this list while in their teams. After this portion of the activity is completed, have the students move into their teams to discuss the names written on the board. Have them decide on one famous person for each person in the group. It then becomes this student's responsibility to locate biographical information about this famous person and to read this information to the group members. Use the forms on pages 103 and 104 to write the information and for student evaluations of the activity.

Next, ask the group members to determine who in their group will be responsible for the biography of one other group member. Each person should both write a biography and be interviewed for one as well. Have the student teams work together in their groups to determine a cover, prepare their rough drafts, edit, make final drafts, and, finally, bind their biographies into a group book. Use the form on page 105 as a springboard for the interview.

To Simplify: Omit the first steps and move directly into the interview and writing process.

To Expand: Have the children make audio or video recordings of their biographical interviews. They may even wish to prepare interviews similar to the kind seen on television magazine shows. Use this recording for Open House or just for fun so that the students can observe themselves in action.

Evaluation: Evaluate individual students by observing them in action with their groups and use the anecdotal record form on page 26 to log this information. Store the forms in the students' portfolios. Then, review each student's written biography.

Processing: Allow time for the student groups to read each other's published work and to view or listen to their audio or visual presentations.

Time of My Life   *The Present*

Biography

My Subject's Name _____

My Name _____

_____

_____

_____

_____

_____

_____

_____

_____

_____

_____

_____

_____

_____

_____

_____

_____

_____

_____

_____

_____

_____

The Present   *Time of My Life*

Time of Your Life Worksheet

Team Name _____

Team Members _____
_____

Each member of your team will be interviewing another team member and writing his or her biography. Before your team begins this process, each member of your team should find a biography of a famous person and read a condensed version of it to your team members.

Write your names and the biographies you will share with your teammates here:

Name   **Biography**

_____   _____
_____   _____
_____   _____
_____   _____

Notice the way the biographies are written.

1. How do they start? _____
_____

2. What are some of the experiences biographers usually tell about?
_____
_____

3. What is the same in the biographies? _____
_____

4. What is different about the biographies? _____
_____
_____

5. From what you have learned, which biography do you like the best?
_____
_____

6. Which famous person do you like the best? _____

7. Why is the person you chose above so appealing to you? _____
_____

Time of My Life *The Present*

Interview Worksheet

Interviewer's Name _____

Subject's Name _____

1. When and where were you born? _____
   _____

2. Do you have brothers and sisters? _____
   _____

3. What is your first memory? _____
   _____

4. What do you like best about your family? _____
   _____

5. What was your happiest day? _____
   _____

6. What was your saddest day? _____
   _____

7. What do you like to do for fun? _____
   _____

8. If you had three wishes, what would you wish for? _____
   _____

9. What would you like to do to make the world a better place? _____
   _____

10. How would you like to be remembered? _____
    _____

Use this space for your own questions.

©1995 Teacher Created Materials, Inc. #651 Cooperative Learning Activities for Language Arts

The Present

Beat the Clock

Purpose: to compete in a dictionary relay race

Skills: using a dictionary; alphabetizing; spelling; teamwork; sportsmanship; organization; decision-making

Materials: copies of pages 107 and 108; one dictionary per student team; writing supplies; one bucket per student team and an additional bucket; a list of pre-selected vocabulary words

Procedure: Explain to the students that each team will be taking part in a dictionary relay race. Each team will need to form a relay, and each member of the team will run to the opposite end of the room, pick a definition slip from the bucket there (upon which you, the teacher, have written a pre-selected vocabulary word), run to the dictionary, look up the word, write the definition on the slip, and place the slip in the team's definition bucket. The team to have defined correctly the most words in a ten-minute time period wins the first leg of the game.

Next, use the collective definition slips to hold a spelling bee. The teams can compete against one another until there is one winner. End the day with a victory party. Serve cookies and punch and award new dictionaries to the winning team members.

To Simplify: Shorten the length of time the teams compete. Omit the spelling bee.

To Expand: Have the students select their own words for a championship spelling bee. Each team places in a bowl twenty words the members have selected. (You may want to specify the number of syllables allowable per word, both the minimum and the maximum.) After all lists have been submitted, make a master list for the teams to use for practice. Hold a grand master spelling bee.

Evaluation: Evaluate individual student performances by using the anecdotal record form on page 26. File the form in each student's portfolio.

Processing: Process with your entire class by discussing the results of the games and how it feels to win or lose. Ask student groups to share their experiences and discuss what they would like to do differently next time. Also ask them how they feel they functioned as a team.

Beat the Clock   *The Present*

"Beat the Clock" Worksheet

Team Name _____

Team Members _____

_____

_____

The object of "Beat the Clock" is to see how many words your team can look up and define in a designated time. You will draw a word to define from a bucket placed across the room, look up the word in the dictionary, define it on your definition slip, and then place the slip in your team's bucket. Use this tally sheet to keep a record of the words you define. Be sure to write each one down as you go along. In case of a mix-up, you will have a written record.

	Player 1 Words	Player 2 Words	Player 3 Words	Player 4 Words	Player 5 Words	Player 6 Words
1.						
2.						
3.						
4.						
5.						
6.						
7.						
8.						
9.						
10.						
11.						
12.						

©1995 Teacher Created Materials, Inc.   #651 Cooperative Learning Activities for Language Arts

The Present   *Beat the Clock*

"Beat the Clock" Definition Slips

Team _____ **Name** _____
Word _____
Definition _____
_____

- -

Team _____ **Name** _____
Word _____
Definition _____
_____

- -

Team _____ **Name** _____
Word _____
Definition _____
_____

- -

Team _____ **Name** _____
Word _____
Definition _____
_____

- -

Team _____ **Name** _____
Word _____
Definition _____
_____

- -

Team _____ **Name** _____
Word _____
Definition _____
_____

The Present

Time Line Mural

Purpose: to create a time-line picture mural

Skills: knowledge of history; fact finding; art; organize; decision-making; consensus

Materials: copies of pages 110–112; large strips of butcher paper and art supplies or a large blackboard and colored chalk; reference texts

Procedure: In this activity, students do research to make an accurate time-line mural. Some teachers may wish to use a chalkboard to make a temporary mural, but some will find that students are disappointed when their artwork is erased. If this is the case, use large strips of butcher paper that can later be made into a colorful bulletin-board display.

Ask the student teams to use the time-line worksheets (pages 110–111) to determine important historical points of reference. If you have used the beginning section of this book, you will wish to remind students of the civilizations studied so that they can be included in their time lines. Have the students choose several important times in history and illustrate only those, or let them illustrate whatever they feel is important.

After the children have completed their worksheets, ask them to make some preliminary sketches. They can use page 112 as a mural model. Once their sketches are complete, they are ready to create their murals.

To Simplify: Have students complete the time-line worksheets and choose only one event to illustrate.

To Expand: Have the students complete school-year time-line murals. Compare the results with the historical time line.

Evaluation: Evaluate murals for historical accuracy. Evaluate individual student performances by using the anecdotal record form on page 26. Store the forms in the students' portfolios.

Processing: Process with your class by discussing and comparing the various murals and deciding which are the most accurate and why. Note the different ways that teams have chosen to illustrate historical events.

The Present   Time Line Mural

"Time-Line Mural" Worksheet

Team Name _____

Team Members _____

_____

_____

Your team will be making a large time-line mural. Before you begin your mural, use this page and the next to plan your time line.

List the ten most important historical events you would like to illustrate.

1.

2.

3.

4.

5.

6.

7.

8.

9.

10.

Time Line Mural   *The Present*

"Time-Line Mural" Worksheet

(cont.)

Use this miniature time line to plan your actual time line.

The year 1

Decide:

Who will be responsible for which of the following tasks?

1. Planners _____
   _____

2. Material gatherers _____
   _____

3. Researchers _____
   _____

4. Artists _____
   _____

©1995 Teacher Created Materials, Inc.   #651 Cooperative Learning Activities for Language Arts

The Present *Time Line Mural*

"Time-Line Mural" Model

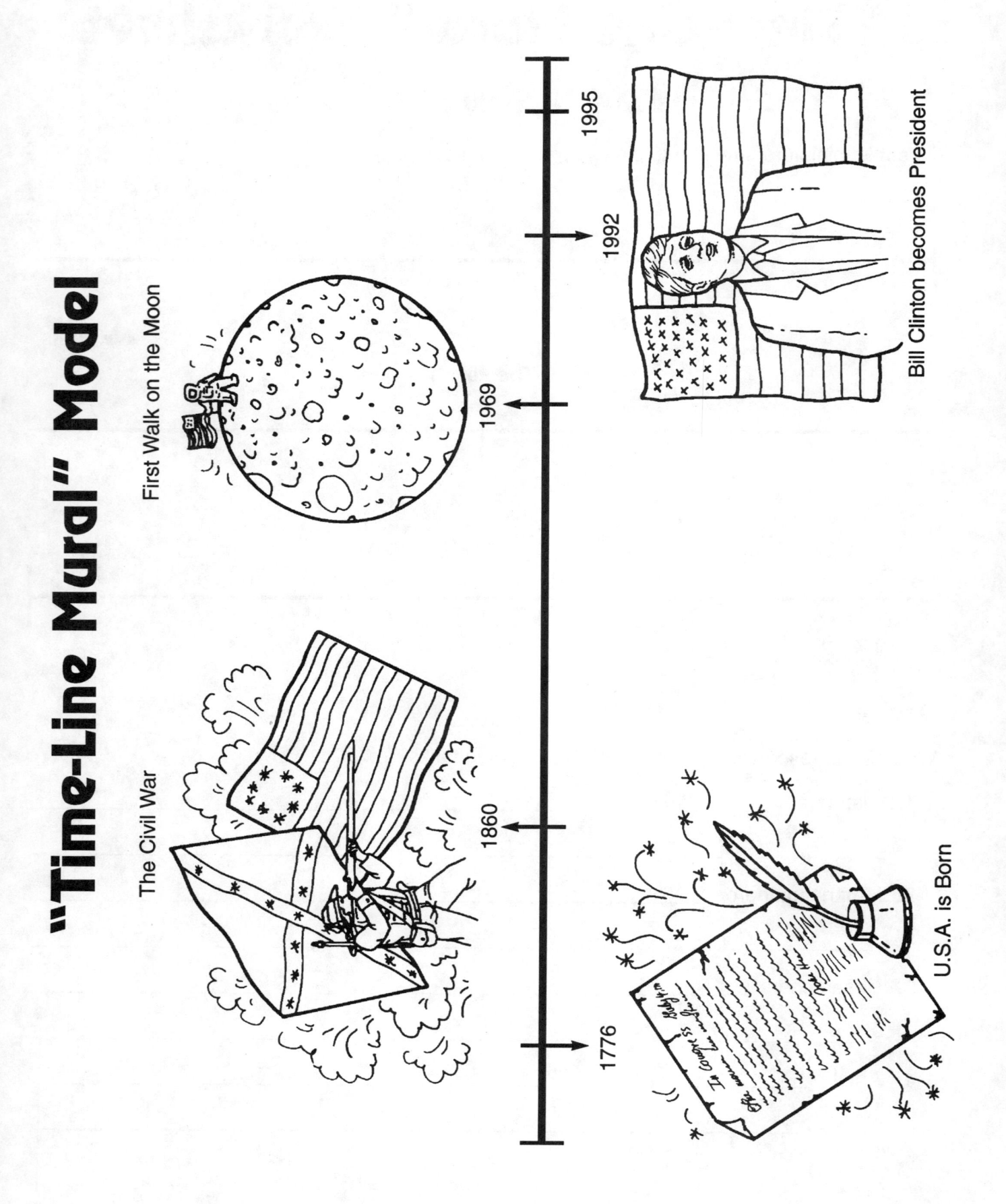

First Walk on the Moon

1995

1992

Bill Clinton becomes President

1969

The Civil War

1860

1776

U.S.A. is Born

#651 Cooperative Learning Activities for Language Arts

The Future

A Note to the Teacher About the Writing Process

This section of *Cooperative Learning for Language Arts* deals with the future. The activities here are designed to take the upper-elementary student through the steps of the writing process. Although these steps may be given a variety of names, they generally follow this sequence:

Step 1—Establishing a Need to Write
Step 2—Brainstorming
Step 3—Organizing Ideas
Step 4—Writing a First Draft
Step 5—Editing
Step 6—Revising/Rewriting
Step 7—Publishing

The editing step may occur many times and may take the form of self-editing, peer-editing, teacher-editing, and so on. Revising is a response to editing and is the option of the writer. Rewriting, or making a final draft, is fairly standard because even the most accomplished professional writer rarely produces a perfect first draft. Publishing has come to mean any way of making a piece of writing available to people other than the writer. A variety of classroom publishing ideas and a list of magazines that publish children's writing can be found on pages 138 through 141.

Of course, some of the steps in the writing process are more readily adapted to cooperative group learning than are others. Interaction in a small group can help learners establish a need to write. It is also a good place to brainstorm. Organizational techniques can be taught and practiced in small groups, but organizing one's own ideas and getting them down on paper in a first draft is really an individual activity. Sharing and peer-editing are made-to-order group activities. Revising and rewriting are private. Publishing is a great group activity because it is essentially a celebration of the work that has been done.

Students in the upper elementary grades should be comfortable enough with cooperative groups to move in and out of them with ease, working as an individual or participating in a large group when appropriate.

This process of writing differs from the traditional method of teaching writing in three notable ways. First, the writing process can stop at any point. The students or teacher can say, "I've gotten what I need from this piece. I'll leave it at this point." Second, students are not expected to produce "perfect" examples of their writing for grading purposes when what they are really doing is producing a first-draft essay for which they had no time to prepare. Third, students are encouraged to learn that writing is a process and to be patient with themselves, to stretch their skills, and to take pride in improving their own work.

The writing process is a real-life approach to teaching students how to write. It replicates the way people really use writing as a life skill and a creative tool.

For student information on the writing process, you may wish to enlarge the next page and display it on your classroom bulletin board or wall. You might also duplicate copies for each student's notebook and portfolio.

One final note—any method of teaching writing depends for its success upon the underlying knowledge base with which students have been provided. No matter the method, the goal is to achieve a piece of writing that communicates effectively and in an interesting manner.

©1995 Teacher Created Materials, Inc.

The Future *A Note to the Teacher About the Writing Process*

What Is the Writing Process?

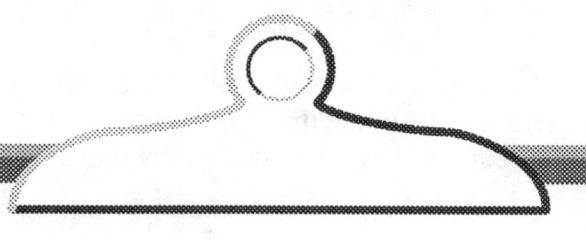

Step 1—Establishing a Need to Write

Step 2—Brainstorming

Step 3—Organizing Ideas

Step 4—Writing a First Draft

Step 5—Editing

Step 6—Revising/Rewriting

Step 7—Publishing

The Future

Providing a Knowledge Base

> **Purpose:** to provide students with information about time capsules, both those that people have discovered and those that people have left for others
>
> **Skills:** reading; writing; listening; thinking (analysis and evaluation); using research materials; speaking; following directions; working in a group
>
> **Materials:** reference materials such as sets of encyclopedias; writing materials; copies of pages 116 and 117

Procedure: Begin the activity by meeting in a whole-class group to consider some questions related to the history of time capsules. Write these questions on the chalkboard.

- What kind of time capsules have been found?
- Were they left on purpose or by accident?
- What made them last until they could be found?
- What has been learned from things that have been found?
- Are our time capsules left on purpose or by accident?
- What kinds of time capsules have people from our civilization left for people on purpose or by accident?
- What will people learn about us from our time capsules?

Send the students to their groups to research and discuss the questions. Have them make notes to bring back to the large group on the "What We Have Found" worksheets on pages 116 and 117.

To Simplify: Read aloud to the students an encyclopedia article on time capsules. Discuss the information. When they go to their groups, have an aide, parent volunteer, or student helper work with them to complete the worksheets.

To Expand: Advanced learners can do community research via the telephone to find out about local buildings that contain time capsules. (Time capsules are sometimes buried under a plaque on a building's cornerstone.) They can take home a letter to parents asking them if they know of any local time capsules.

Evaluation: Evaluate this activity by spending time with each group as they consult research materials and discuss what they find. Make any appropriate notes on the anecdotal record form on page 26. These forms can later be added to the students' portfolios.

Processing: Process with the class by having student representatives from each group read their group's worksheets. Discuss the information they found and the conclusions they reached.

The Future   *Providing a Knowledge Base*

"What We Have Found" Worksheet

Team Name _____

Team Members _____

_____

_____

Look in reference books and discuss the information you find. Then, write what you think on the lines below.

1. What kind of "time capsules" were left for us by ancient people such as the Egyptians?

2. Were they left on purpose or by accident?

3. What made them last so long?

4. What have we learned from the things in these "time capsules"?

Providing a Knowledge Base *The Future*

"What We Have Found" Worksheet (cont.)

5. What kind of time capsules have people in the United States left for people in the future?

6. Have all of our time capsules been left on purpose?

7. What have people done to make sure the things they put in the time capsules will last a long time?

8. What will the things the people of today have put in time capsules tell the people of the future about us?

The Future

Establishing a Need to Write: Making a Time Capsule

> **Purpose:** to think about and discuss the future; to motivate students to write a meaningful message to the future; to learn about time capsules
>
> **Skills:** reading and listening comprehension; oral and written communication; thinking skills
>
> **Materials:** copies of page 119; writing materials; large piece of chart paper taped to the chalkboard; marking pens

Procedure: Begin the activity in a whole-class group. Find out what the students already know about time capsules by asking questions like these:

- What are time capsules?
- Where might some of them be found?
- What qualities should the capsule itself have?
- Why do people make time capsules?
- Have you ever seen an article in the newspaper about a time capsule? (Watch for one and bring it to school to share.)

Read aloud to the class about time capsules to fill in the gaps in their knowledge. Tell students they will be going to their cooperative groups to talk about some of the reasons that people make time capsules. They will also be discussing the physical qualities a time capsule should have. Ask students to complete page 119 as they discuss these issues.

While students discuss time capsules in their groups, walk around the room to answer questions and give any necessary input. When all have completed the worksheet, have them come back to the large group to share their ideas. As the groups share, write the reasons people make time capsules at the top of the chart paper and the physical qualities of good time capsules on the lower part of the chart paper.

To Simplify: Give the students much more information at the beginning of the lesson. Look up "time capsule" in *The Reader's Guide to Periodical Literature* and find some information about contemporary time capsules—either their burial or their discovery. The worksheet will then become a way to check on listening comprehension and recall of information.

To Expand: Assign students the task of finding information in *The Reader's Guide to Periodical Literature*. Make going to the library and looking up information a homework assignment.

Evaluation: Evaluate both the ideas generated by the students and the way they worked together to generate them. Make any appropriate notes on the anecdotal record form (page 26), which can later be added to the students' portfolios.

Processing: Process with the whole class. Ask questions such as these: Why do you think we have been discussing time capsules? What do you think the world will be like fifty years from now? What might it be like one-hundred years from now? Is there anything about the world we live in that you would like to tell the people of the future? Would you like to tell them what you think they will be like, how they will live, or what they will eat and wear?

Establishing a Need to Write: Making a Time Capsule 	*The Future*

Team Name _____

Team Members_____
_____
_____

Time Capsule Questions

As you discuss the reasons people make time capsules and the physical characteristics a good time capsule should have, write your ideas in the appropriate spaces below.

The Reasons People Make Time Capsules

1.

2.

3.

4.

5.

The Physical Characteristics of a Good Time Capsule

1.

2.

3.

4.

5.

©1995 Teacher Created Materials, Inc.   119   #651 Cooperative Learning Activities for LANGUAGE ARTS

The Future

Brainstorming: My Message to the Future

> **Purpose:** to determine a variety of ways in which letters might be placed in a time capsule
>
> **Skills:** listening; speaking; thinking; writing; following directions
>
> **Materials:** copies of pages 121 and 122; writing and drawing materials

Procedure: Start this activity in the large group. Go over the results of the previous activity (pages 118 and 119). Discuss the reasons the students decided that people might want to make a time capsule. Discuss how a letter to the future might fit into these reasons. (Students may suggest that they could describe themselves, the house they live in, their city or school, the technology they use, and methods of transportation and communication, or they may look at it the other way around and write a letter telling what they think the future will be like and why it might be that way.)

This is a good time for students to go to their small groups. If you have aides or parent volunteers who can remember to accept each suggestion, no matter how wild or how dull, and do so in a nonjudgmental manner, include them in your plans. Have each group choose a student secretary to record (with the help of the aide or volunteer) the ideas generated by the group on the "Small-Group Brainstorming Form" (page 121).

To Simplify: Give students more suggestions and more time for large-group discussion about what they could write in a letter to the future. Then, make yourself very available as questions arise in small groups.

To Expand: Have students think of themselves as the future. What kind of letter would they enjoy getting from a child who lived one-hundred years ago? Why? Discuss.

Evaluation: Evaluate the brainstorming process by spending time with each small group. This is also a good time to take a look at group skills. Are the students polite and positive in their comments to one another? Are they remembering to give compliments? Make any appropriate notes on the anecdotal record form (page 26), which can later be added to the students' portfolios.

Processing: Process with the whole class by having the groups read their lists of ideas to the large group. Choose someone to consolidate all of the ideas on the "Whole-Class Brainstorming Form" (page 122) or ask a parent helper to do it. You will want to make copies of the whole-class list for students to refer to later.

Brainstorming: My Message to the Future **The Future**

Team Name _____

Team Members _____
_____
_____

Small-Group Brainstorming Form

Write your ideas for the topic on the lines below.

Topic: My Message to the Future

_____
_____
_____
_____
_____
_____
_____
_____
_____
_____
_____
_____
_____
_____
_____
_____

The Future *Brainstorming: My Message to the Future*

Whole-Class Brainstorming Form

The teacher can use one copy of this form to consolidate the ideas generated by the small groups and recorded on the "Small-Group Brainstorming Form" (page 121). Then, make a copy of the whole list for each student.

Topic: My Message to the Future

_____
_____
_____
_____
_____
_____
_____
_____
_____
_____
_____
_____
_____
_____
_____
_____
_____
_____
_____
_____
_____
_____

The Future

Organizing Ideas

Purpose: to teach students several methods for organizing their ideas before writing; to practice thinking skills

Skills: reading; writing; listening; thinking; speaking; following directions; coming to consensus

Materials: copies of pages 124–129; writing materials

Procedure: Begin the activity in a whole-class group by telling students that they will be learning and/or reviewing several ways to organize their ideas before writing. Copy the skeletons of the various samples (pages 124, 126, and 128) on the chalkboard. Fill in the middle box in the "Clustering Sample." Ask the students to read this title. Then, ask them to generate ideas to go in the ovals.

Next, fill in the title of the "Outlining Sample." Ask the students to generate possible main topics and sub-topics. (Use the sample for suggestions if the students get stuck.)

Now, fill in the title of the "Venn Diagram Sample." Ask the students when this type of organizer would be helpful. Assign one or more appropriate subjects and have the students go to their cooperative groups. They should use the forms on pages 125, 127, and 129 to organize and record their ideas about the subject(s). Some ideas for subjects are the continents, television shows, sports, desert animals, forest animals, undersea life, and types of transportation.

To Simplify: Have students work through these organizers with the aid of a helper who can fill in forms drawn on the chalkboard while students offer suggestions and record the information on their own forms.

To Expand: Advanced students can complete several of each type of organizer using topics you assign or topics they choose themselves.

Evaluation: Evaluate this activity by spending time with each group and by looking at their completed forms. Make any appropriate notes on the anecdotal record forms (page 26), which can later be added to the students' portfolios.

Processing: Process with the whole class by having a group representative from each team take turns reading their organizers aloud. Pass out more forms. Tell the students they can begin to organize their ideas for the upcoming homework assignment (a letter to the future). This organization should be ready for the next activity.

The Future   *Organizing Ideas*

Clustering Sample

Draw this sample on the chalkboard and write the title in the central box. Ask students to determine the information to put in the ovals. Use the information from the sample if they get stuck.

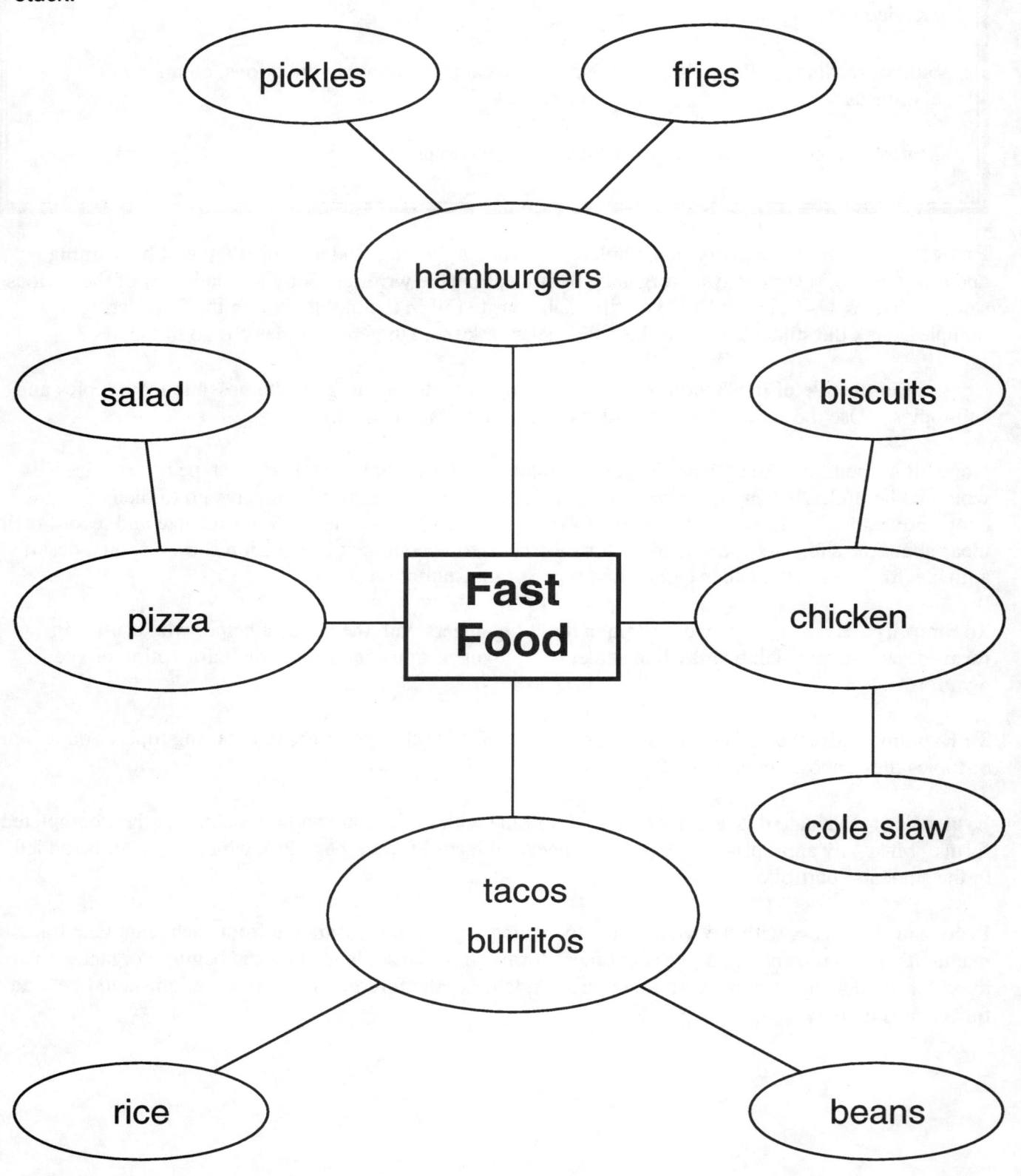

- Fast Food
  - hamburgers
    - pickles
    - fries
  - pizza
    - salad
  - chicken
    - biscuits
    - cole slaw
  - tacos / burritos
    - rice
    - beans

Organizing Ideas   *The Future*

Clustering Form

Give students this form to practice clustering information.

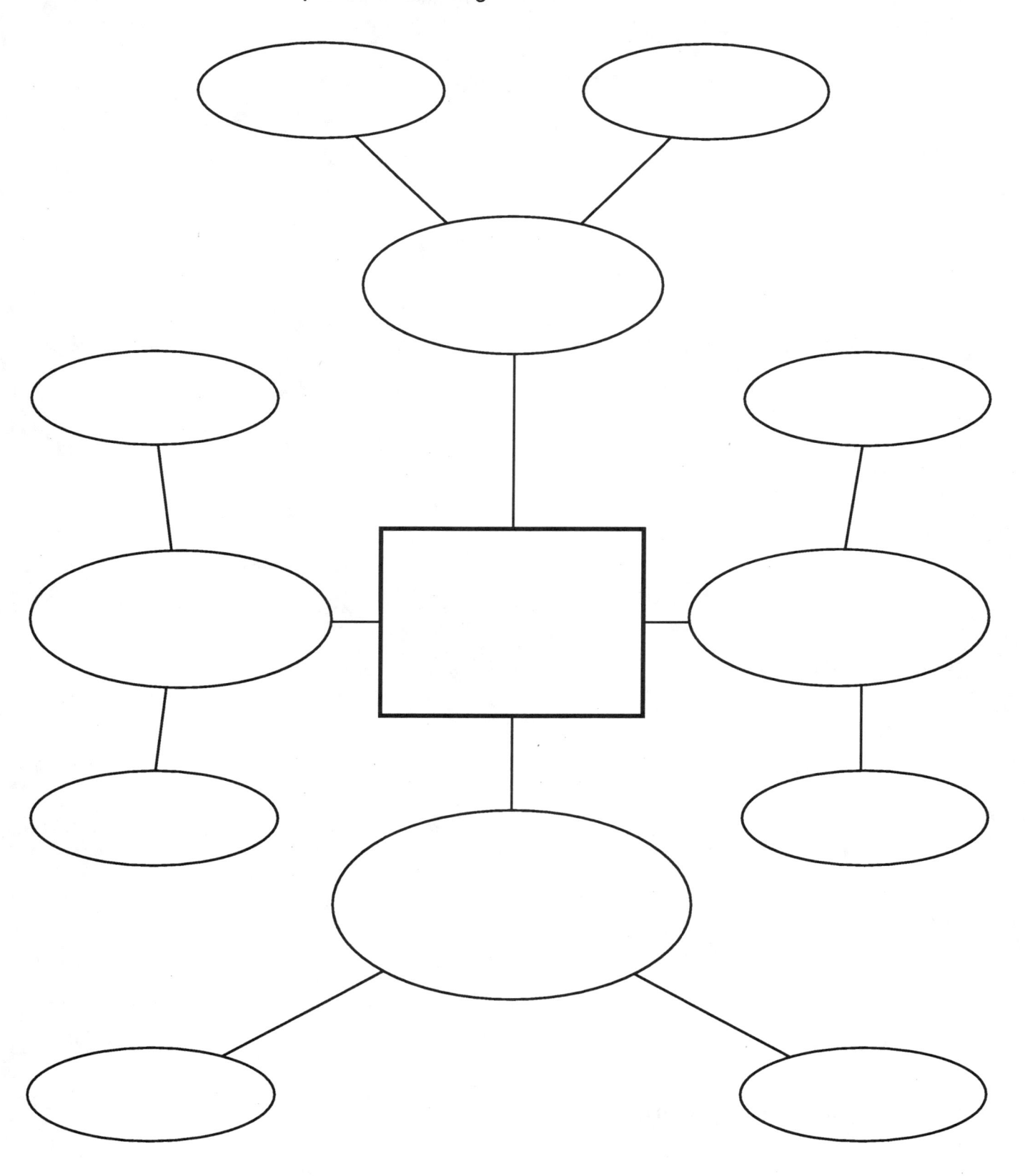

The Future   *Organizing Ideas*

Outlining Sample

Draw this sample on the chalkboard and write in the title of the outline. Ask students to determine topics and subtopics. Use the information from the sample if they get stuck.

Title of Outline: **Oceans of the World**

I. Atlantic Ocean

    A. location

    B. size

    C. surrounding countries

II. Pacific Ocean

    A. location

    B. size

    C. surrounding countries

III. Indian Ocean

    A. location

    B. size

    C. surrounding countries

IV. Arctic Ocean

    A. location

    B. size

    C. surrounding countries

Organizing Ideas   *The Future*

Outlining Form

Give students this form to practice outlining information.

Title of Outline: _____

I.

    A.

    B.

    C.

II.

    A.

    B.

    C.

III.

    A.

    B.

    C.

IV.

    A.

    B.

    C.

The Future *Organizing Ideas*

Venn Diagram Sample

Draw this sample on the chalkboard and write in the title of the diagram. Ask students to determine the information for the parts of the diagram. Use the information from the sample if they get stuck.

Title of Diagram: **Basketball and Football**

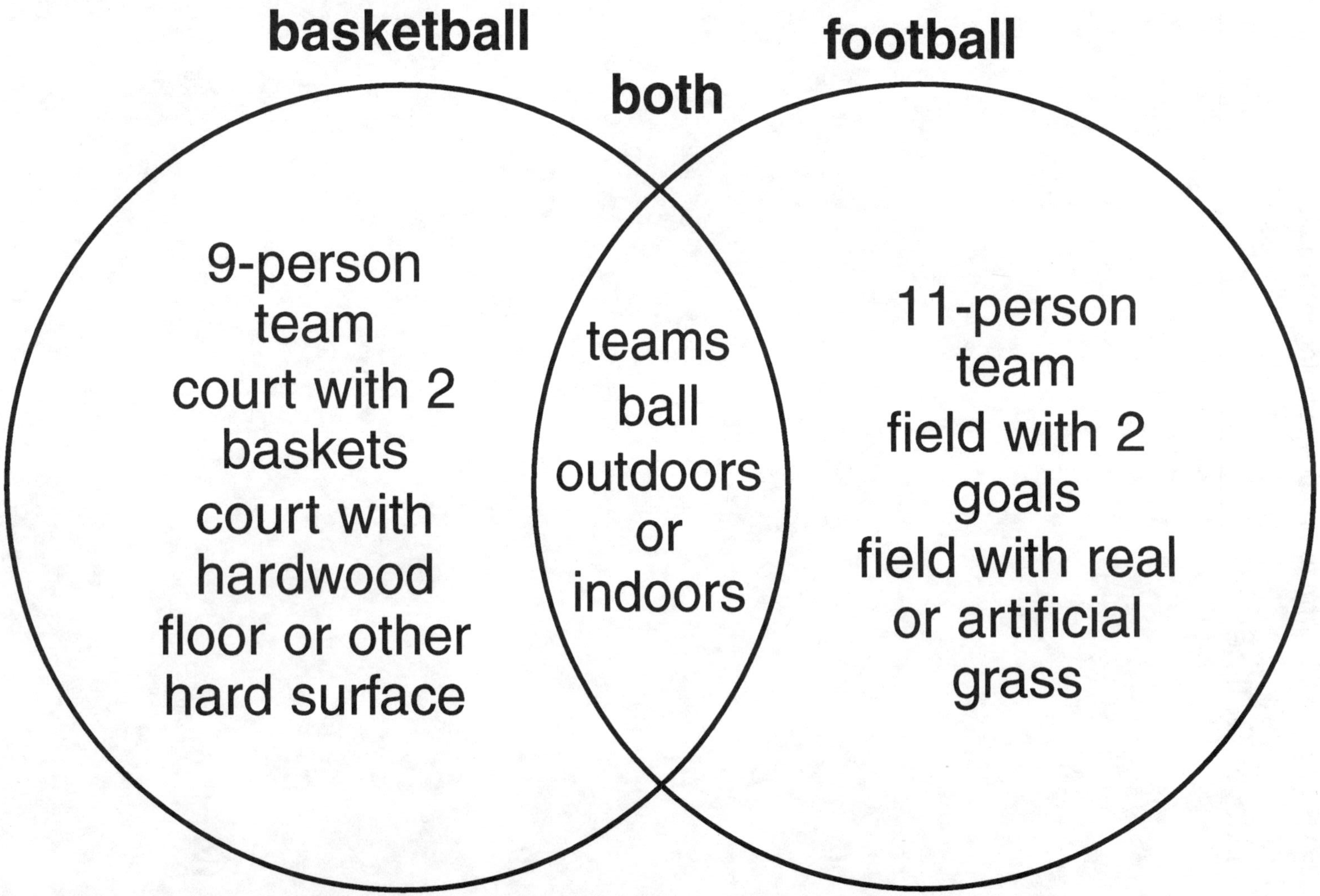

football

- 11-person team
- field with 2 goals
- field with real or artificial grass

both

- teams
- ball
- outdoors or indoors

basketball

- 9-person team
- court with 2 baskets
- court with hardwood floor or other hard surface

Organizing Ideas | *The Future*

Venn Diagram Form

Give students this form to practice making a Venn diagram.

Title of Diagram: _____

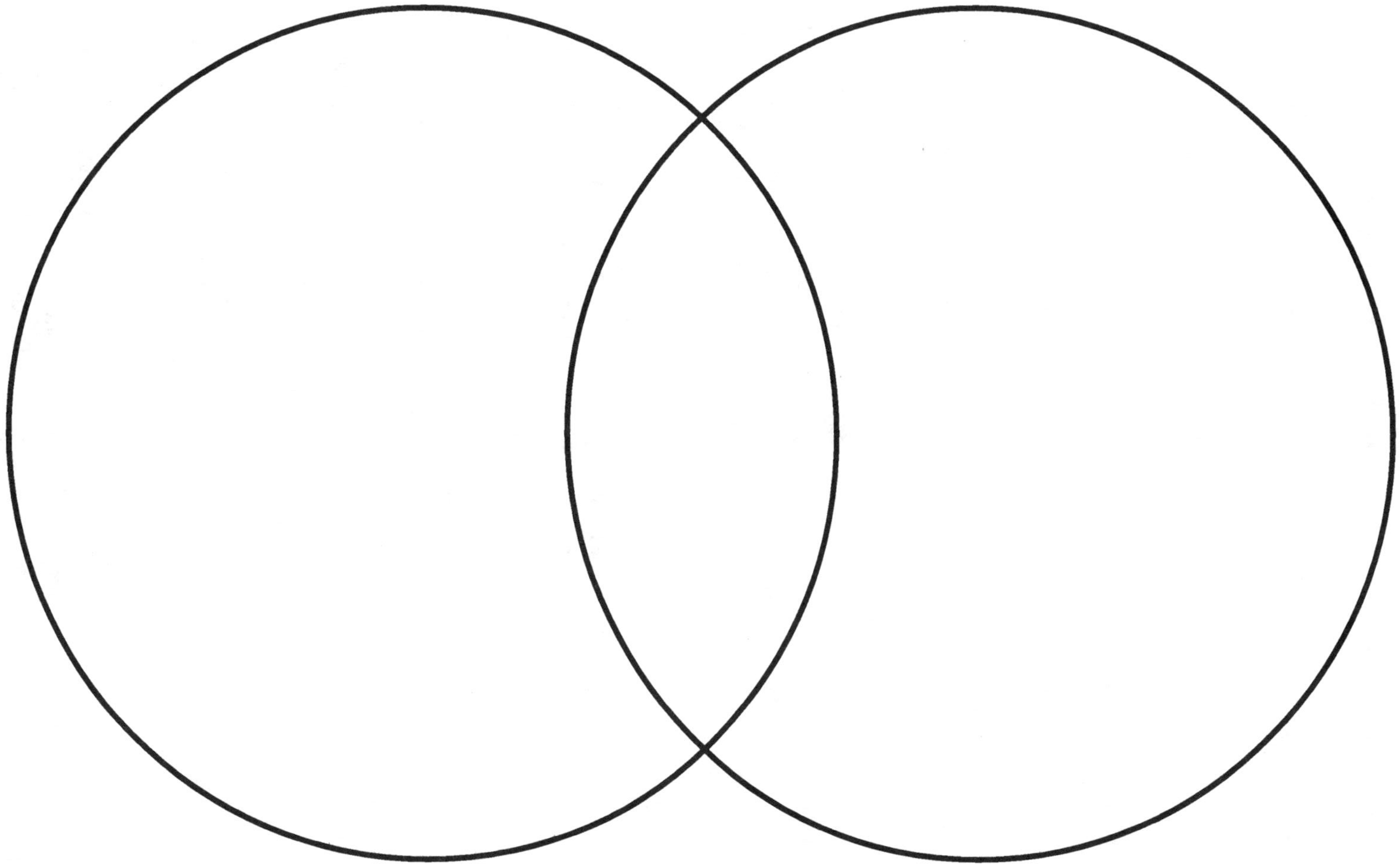

The Future

Writing and Sharing the First Draft

Purpose: to give students the opportunity to get their ideas on paper and then share them with a positive, receptive audience

Skills: reading; writing; listening; thinking; speaking; having a positive attitude toward peers; following directions; working in a group

Materials: copies of pages 131 and 132; writing materials

Procedure: Begin the activity in a whole-class group. Tell the students they will be writing the first draft of their letter to the future. Review the ideas that were generated in the brainstorming session.

Remind students that first drafts are not supposed to be perfect. They should get their ideas on paper without worrying about spelling, capitals, periods, and so forth. (This means that you will not supply information while they are writing.) They should write as much as they can, because they can always take out things later if they decide to do so. Tell them they can use any of their organizing forms to help them. Give them ample time to write and an independent activity to turn to if they finish before the others.

Later in the day, tell the students they will have an opportunity to read their first drafts to one another in their groups. Remind them about being positive listeners. Show them the "Compliments" pages (pages 131 and 132) and tell them they will each have a set. They will cut the compliments apart and hand them to their group members as the stories are read. The teacher will also hand out compliment slips.

To Simplify: Students who have trouble getting their ideas on paper should, if at all possible, work with a helper who will give them confidence rather than too much help.

To Expand: Advanced students can write their own more specific compliments on the backs of the compliment slips before they hand them out.

Evaluation: Evaluate this activity by spending time with each group, listening to the stories as students read them aloud, and observing the behavior of the rest of the group. Make any appropriate notes on the anecdotal record forms (page 26). These can be added to the students' portfolios.

Processing: Process with the whole class by asking students how they felt about getting their ideas down on paper, reading their first drafts aloud to the small group, and receiving and giving compliments. What was the hardest part for them? What was the easiest part? What would they do differently if they were to do it over?

Writing and Sharing the First Draft *The Future*

Compliments

Cut these compliment slips apart and hand them to the other members of your group after each reads his or her first draft aloud.

Great Story!	GOOD JOB!
Thank you for sharing!	I never got bored!
I learned something new!	TOO COOL
VERY ENTERTAINING	I enjoyed this!

The Future — Writing and Sharing the First Draft

Compliments (cont.)

WOW! WOW! WOW!	**You really held my attention!**
Fabulous ideas!	**I LIKE YOUR STORY!**
WOW! Great Vocabulary!	**INTERESTING IDEAS**
SUPER SUPER SUPER	**FANTASTIC!**

The Future

Peer Editing, Revising, and Rewriting

> **Purpose:** to provide an opportunity to use peer editing; to revise, rewrite, and produce a final draft
>
> **Skills:** reading; writing; listening; thinking (analysis and evaluation); speaking; following directions
>
> **Materials:** copies of first drafts; differently colored pen or pencil for each group member; one dictionary per group; several grammar textbooks per group; writing materials

Procedure: Begin the activity in a whole-class group by telling students that they will be doing peer editing. Review the meaning of the words "peer" and "editing." Explain that you have made copies of everyone's first draft so no one's original work will be written on.

Review the "read around" process. Each person in the group passes his paper to the left (or right—just as long as it is the same direction). Each person reads the story that has been passed and makes positive comments and/or corrections right on the paper in his or her own color of pen or pencil. Everyone writes with a different color so the person who wrote the story will know who to ask about each comment or correction. When everyone is through with the first paper, everyone passes the papers the same way again at the same time. The process ends when each person has his or her own paper back.

Explain that there is only one focus during a peer-editing session. In this first session, students will look at only one of the following: capitals, periods, verb agreement, verb tense, spelling, or clarity of expression. They will not comment on anything else. Each person will use appropriate reference books to help with this activity. (This activity can be repeated as many times as you wish, targeting something different each time.)

Call the students back to the big group after all peer-editing rounds have been completed. Explain to the students that they will now be working individually. They may now revise and rewrite, taking under consideration those suggestions that appeal to them. When they are satisfied with their work, they may make final copies of their letters.

To Simplify: To simplify the peer-editing activity, students can try to process first with a partner and a parent volunteer or classroom aide.

To Expand: Advanced learners can, as a group, discuss and evaluate the suggested corrections and decide whether or not to make the changes.

Evaluation: Evaluate this activity by spending time with each group and also by looking at the editing comments they are making. Make any appropriate notes on the anecdotal record form (page 26). Be sure to add these to the students' portfolios. Evaluate the finished letters, using a rubric that measures those qualities you are addressing in your writing program.

Processing: Process with the whole class by having students comment on the ways they felt while having other students edit their work and while they edited the work of others. Which was more difficult? What would they like to focus on the next time they do peer editing? What part of the peer-editing process helped them the most with their revisions?

The Future

Completing the Time Capsule

Purpose: to decide what the capsule itself will be made of and what will go inside

Skills: oral communication (listening and speaking); thinking (analysis and evaluation); following directions; making decisions

Materials: writing materials; each student's completed letter; scratch copies of the chart on page 135; permanent copies of the chart on page 135; artifacts to be decided upon

Procedure: Meet with the whole class. Discuss the time capsule and come to a final decision about what you will use (e.g., commercially-designed time capsule, sealed glass jar, thermos jar or bottle, etc.) and who will be responsible for getting it. (It is fine for the teacher to do this.)

Tell the students that each of them will be bringing an "artifact" to put in the capsule along with their letters. Write the following requirements for artifacts on the chalkboard.

- *Artifacts must be very small.*

- *Each artifact must have something to do with the letter to which it is attached.*
  (A student who writes a description of himself/herself may want to include a picture. A student who describes what entertainment is like might include a movie or television listing from the newspaper. A student who has predicted the future should enclose an original drawing to go with it.)

- *Artifacts must be available within a few days.*
  (A student who would like to include a small shell, for example, must be able to get one before the time capsule is scheduled to be "published.")

Have students go to their small groups to discuss their ideas and decide upon their artifacts. They can fill in the information on their scratch copy of page 135.

To Simplify: An aide or older student can help students in a small group think of artifacts and make decisions.

To Expand: Advanced learners can enter their stories in a computer and print them (or simply type them) and send them off to a publisher or a writing contest. See page 141.

Evaluation: Evaluate this activity by spending time with each group. Ask for rationales for artifacts. Back in the large group, collect the scratch charts and consolidate the information (alphabetical order by student name will make it more useful). Collect all letters to copy for inclusion in the students' portfolios along with any notes on the anecdotal record forms (page 26).

Processing: Process with the whole class. Ask them how they felt about sending a message to the future.

Completing the Time Capsule *The Future*

The Capsule and What Goes in It

Make enough copies of the chart below so you have an entry space for each student. Then, fill in the information. Include one whole-class chart in the time capsule and keep one as a record.

Student Name	Topic of Letter	Associated Artifact

The Future

Publishing the Time Capsule

Purpose: to consider methods of "publishing" a time capsule and decide upon the most appropriate one; to design, write, and perform a ceremony; to make and keep records of what was done; to decide when the capsule will be opened

Skills: oral communication (listening and speaking); thinking (analysis, synthesis, and evaluation); following directions; delegating responsibilities; making decisions; reaching consensus

Materials: writing materials

Procedure: Meet with the whole class. Discuss ways in which a time capsule can be published. (The most common ways are by burying it, hiding it, or leaving it with someone who will follow your instructions about what to do with it.) No matter which method of publishing is chosen, a ceremony is almost always held to mark the event, and a time must be chosen for opening the capsule. This is sometimes far in the future, but it can also be on an important date for the people who made it. Students, for example, might choose the following:

- Publish their time capsule by leaving both it and the instructions about what to do with it with a teacher they trust.

- Have a ceremony at the last assembly of the school year.

- Leave it with a teacher with instructions to produce it when their class graduates from a certain grade. (If they make the time capsule in the fourth grade, they may want it to be a part of their elementary school graduation. If they make it during sixth grade, they may want it produced when they graduate from middle school, junior high, or high school.)

Have students go to their small groups to discuss their ideas and make up their minds. When everyone is ready, come back to the large group, make a list of the options the students suggest, and clarify them through discussion. Later, list the options on the ballot form (page 137), make copies for the students, and vote later in the day or the next day.

To Simplify: An aide or older student can help students in a small group think of options.

To Expand: Advanced learners can discuss the possibility of making personal time capsules that might become part of a birthday celebration.

Evaluation: Evaluate this activity by spending time with each group. Answer questions on what various options would involve. Back in the large group, ask representatives to read their group's suggestions for publishing, the ceremony, and the opening.

Processing: Process with the whole class. Did groups have a hard time making these decisions? Why?

Publishing the Time Capsule   *The Future*

Time Capsule Options Ballot

The teacher will write in the options chosen by the class before making copies for voting.

Method of Publishing
(Choose one.)

☐ _____

☐ _____

☐ _____

Type of Ceremony
(Choose one.)

☐ _____

☐ _____

☐ _____

Date and Occasion to Open
(Choose one.)

☐ _____

☐ _____

☐ _____

The Future

Other Publishing Ideas

Have you ever . . .

worn it on a t-shirt? . . . asked to tack it to a community bulletin board? . . . served it on a platter? . . . sung it with a guitar? . . . framed it? . . . read it aloud? . . . had it published in a parents' newsletter? . . . written it in watercolor? . . . taped it as a radio program? . . . sent it to a local newspaper? . . . bound it in a book? . . . hung it in your room? . . . performed it for an assembly? . . . written it in fresh snow? . . . read it in a poetry parade? . . . sent it to a nursing home? . . . read it over the school's public address system? . . . written it in a cookbook? . . . received permission to draw it on a graffiti mural? . . . sent it to a sick classmate? . . . written it to a penpal? . . . told it to a pet? . . . presented it in an animated film or comic strip? . . . written it in chalk on your sidewalk or driveway? . . . made a poster of it? . . . entered it in a contest? . . . flown it across the room in a paper airplane? . . . stitched it on fabric? . . . written it on an original calendar you have tried to sell? . . . performed it in a puppet show? . . . bound it and placed it in the library? . . . sent it in a letter to a published author? . . . made it a message in a bottle? . . . written it in sand? . . . sent it to a political figure? . . . performed it as a skit in the shopping mall? . . .submitted it to a magazine? . . . read it to a school employee? . . . written it in marker on a poster board? . . . mailed it to a former teacher? . . . saved it in a time capsule for the future? . . . sent it in a class mailbox? . . . illustrated it for a valentine? . . . read it to your class? . . . included it in a writer's showcase bulletin board? . . . tucked it away to be read and enjoyed when you are older?

The Future

Other Publishing Ideas (cont.)

Simple Book Binding

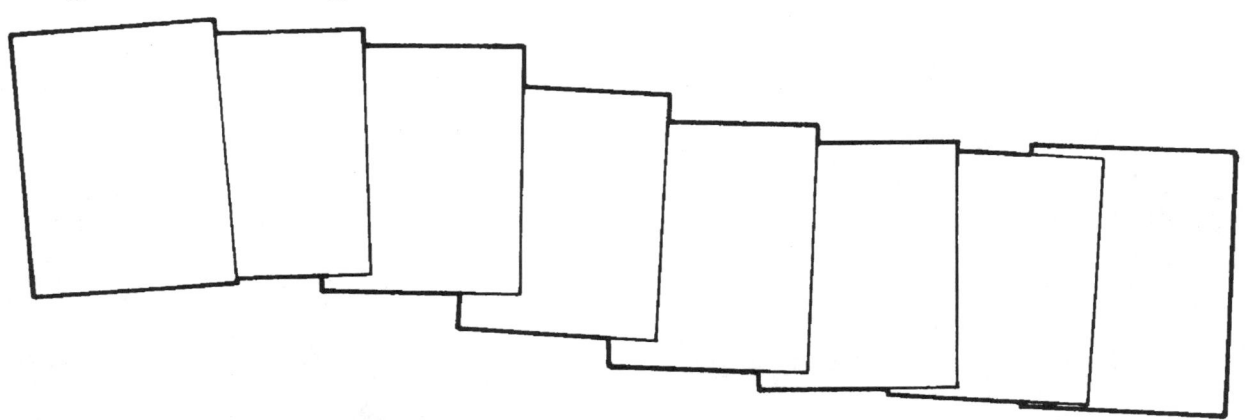

1. Put all pages in order. (The covers should be a little larger than the rest.)

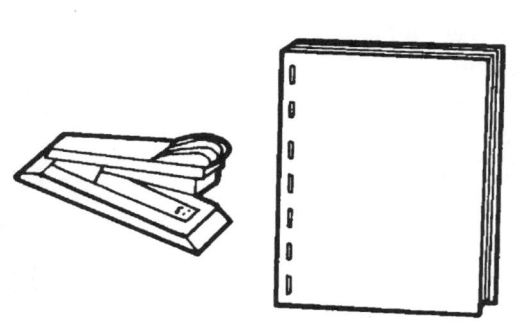

2. Staple the pages together along the left margin.

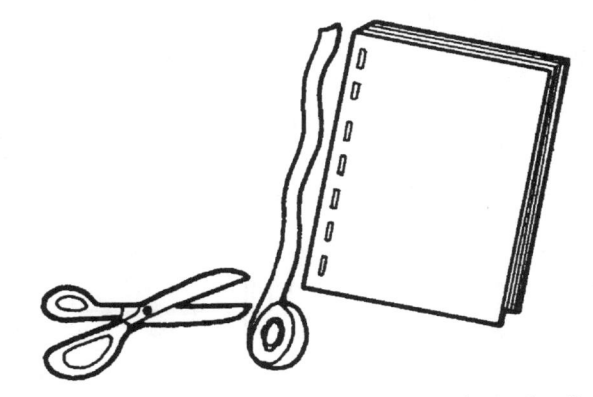

3. Cut book-binding tape to the exact length of the book.

4. Run the center line of the tape along the left side of the book. Fold to cover the front left margin and the back right margin.

©1995 Teacher Created Materials, Inc. 139 #651 Cooperative Learning Activities for Language Arts

The Future

Other Publishing Ideas (cont.)

Hinged Covers

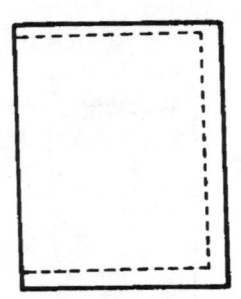

1. Cut the front and back covers slightly larger than the book's pages.

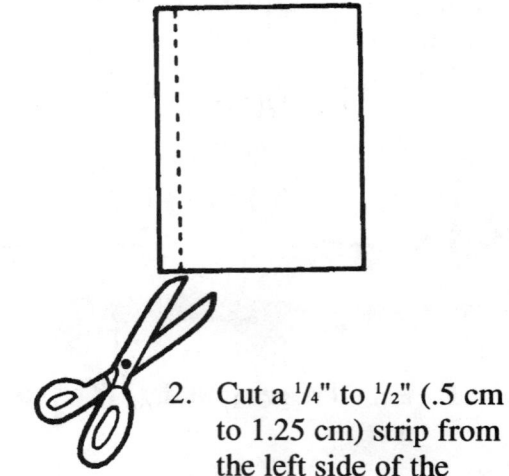

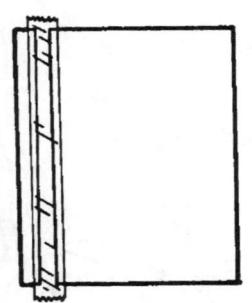

2. Cut a ¼" to ½" (.5 cm to 1.25 cm) strip from the left side of the front cover.

3. Tape the two pieces together again, leaving a narrow opening between the two. Use regular adhesive tape or another very flexible tape.

4. Staple or glue the book's pages and cover together.

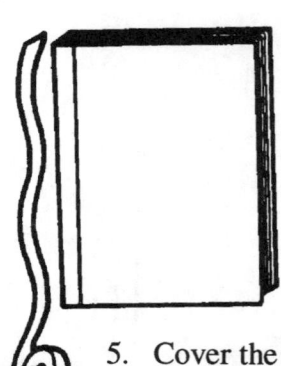

5. Cover the hinge and staples with book-binding tape, wide enough so the hinge and opening do not show.

The Future

Other Publishing Ideas (cont.)

Real Markets for Student Writing

Student writing can be sent to the following addresses. Check your professional journals for more sources.

Children's Playmate (ages 5–8)
P.O. Box 567B
Indianapolis, Indiana 46206

Cricket (ages 6–12)
Cricket League
P.O. Box 300
Peru, Illinois 61354

Ebony Jr! (ages 6–12)
820 S. Michigan Street
Chicago, Illinois 60605

Flying Pencil Press (ages 8–14)
P.O. Box 7667
Elgin, Illinois 60121

Highlights for Children (ages 2–11)
803 Church Street
Honesdale, Pennsylvania 18431

Jack and Jill (ages 8–12)
P.O. Box 567B
Indianapolis, Indiana 46206

Stone Soup (ages 5–14)
P.O. Box 83
Santa Cruz, CA 95063

National Written and Illustrated by . . .
(This is an awards contest for students in all grade levels. Write for rules and guidelines.)
Landmark Editions, Inc.
P.O. Box 4469
Kansas City, Missouri 64127

Cooperative Learning Award

This award is presented to

_____

for

outstanding achievement in

Cooperative Learning

_____
Teacher

_____
Date

Answer Key

Page 29: Time Scale

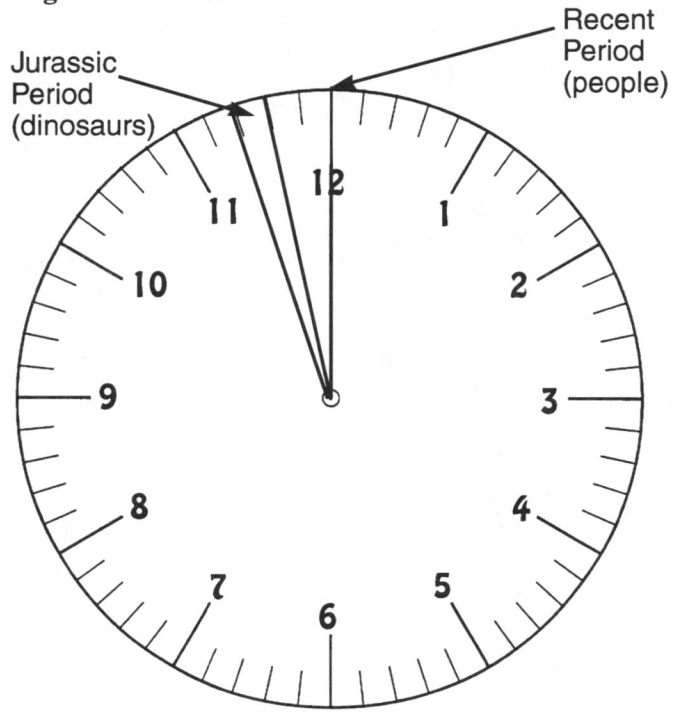

(A clock face diagram showing the Jurassic Period (dinosaurs) and Recent Period (people) as hands pointing near the 12.)

Page 30: Dinowords

(These are possible solutions. The students' answers may vary.)

1. Scientists know Tyrannosaurus Rex ran very fast.
2. Stegosaurus was a herbivore.
3. Allosaurus was carnivorous.
4. We learn about dinosaurs from their fossils.
5. Dinosaurs became extinct for unknown reasons.
6. A new theory says dinosaurs were the ancestors of birds.
7. The study of prehistoric animals is very interesting to most people.

Page 63: Middle Ages Wordsearch

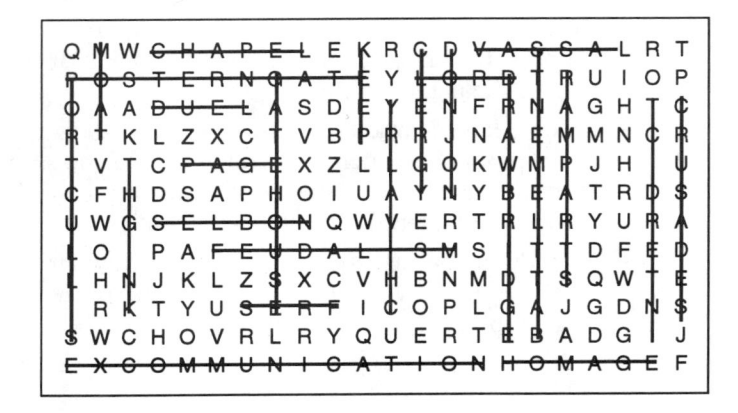

(Word search grid with the following words circled: CHAPEL, VASSAL, POSTERN GATE, LORD, DUEL, KNIGHT, PAGE, CRUSADES, NOBLES, BEAR, FEUDALISM, MOAT, FEUDAL, SERF, BADGE, EXCOMMUNICATION, HOMAGE)

©1995 Teacher Created Materials, Inc.   143   #651 Cooperative Learning Activities for Language Arts

Answer Key (cont.)

Pages 64–65: Definition Worksheet

1. **battlements**—the part of the high, thick outside walls of the castle that face outward, with slits to aim and shoot arrows through
2. **chapel**—small private church inside the castle walls
3. **chivalry**—social code that governed the relationships among people, especially the relationship between knights and their lord; also dictated manners
4. **clergy**—men of the church; priests and bishops (Many members of the clergy owned a great deal of land and were rich and powerful.)
5. **Crusades**—holy wars fought to save the Holy Land (Jerusalem) from the Muslims and the Jews
6. **donjon**—towerlike structure, 50–60 feet (15–18 meters) tall, with thick walls; the strongest part of the castle, built to be easily defended; doubled as a residence for the feudal lord and his family
7. **drawbridge**—bridge that could be raised and lowered; laid across the moat
8. **duel**—a formal fight to the death between two people; considered convenient and honorable; might be ordered by a feudal court to settle an argument; believed that God would give victory to the right side
9. **excommunication**—the act of cutting a person off from the Church and, therefore, from any hope of going to heaven
10. **feudalism**—the system by which a man bound himself to a powerful lord and/or to the land in exchange for the lord's protection
11. **gatehouse**—a fortified structure built around the main gate
12. **homage**—a ceremony in which a knight pledged his life and loyalty to his lord or in which a lord pledged loyalty to a king
13. **interdict**—a decree from the Church that extended a lord's excommunication to all the people on his land (No one could be married, baptized, or buried by the Church. The effect on the people was so bad that the lord usually gave in to the Church.)
14. **keep**—donjon
15. **knight**—man who trained from boyhood to become a warrior and dedicated his life to his lord
16. **lord**—powerful landowner who had the loyalty of his knights and protected the peasants in exchange for their land and their labor; a noble
17. **moat**—deep, water-filled ditch surrounding a castle; could be crossed by lowering the drawbridge
18. **noble**—member of the noble class; a rich, powerful landowner; a lord
19. **page**—young boy who trained to be a knight
20. **portcullis**—armored gate protecting the main entrance of a castle
21. **postern gate**—back gate of the castle; escape route
22. **ramparts**—flat top of the outer wall where men could find shelter behind the battlements
23. **serf**—a person who bound himself to a lord in exchange for protection; a peasant bound to the land
24. **vassal**—a lord who swore loyalty to a stronger lord or to a king

Pages 116–117: "What We Have Found" Worksheet

1. The ancient Egyptians buried treasures with their pharaohs. They also buried everyday articles to make them comfortable in the afterlife. They put these things in sealed rooms in the pyramids.
2. They were left on purpose, but as supplies for the afterlife and not as time capsules.
3. The things buried in Egypt lasted a very long time because of the hot, dry climate and because they were not discovered and stolen by thieves.
4. We have learned a great deal about how the Egyptians dressed, what they ate, and what was important to them.
5. People in the United States have put together many time capsules, buried them underground, and even sent them into space. Many different things have been put into the capsules.
6. People have left many time capsules on purpose but have probably also left many by accident. Things that are thrown away and buried in dumps, for instance, can last a long time and tell a great deal about people.
7. People have learned that things will last longer in airproof and waterproof containers. Time capsules are made of the latest kinds of protective materials.
8. The things put in time capsules will tell about how we lived, what we looked like, and what was important to us.